Auracle's Colour Therapy

"The Power of Love Through Colour"

Order this book online at www.trafford.com
or email orders@trafford.com

Most Trafford titles are also available at major online book retailers.

Print information available on the last page.

ISBN: 978-1-4251-1977-5 (sc)

Trafford rev. 02/17/2023

www.trafford.com
North America & international
toll-free: 844-688-6899 (USA & Canada)
fax: 812 355 4082

Dedications

This is a loving message to all of my Guides, Angels, Archangels, Masters, Ascended Masters and all Light Beings in the Universe who have been with me throughout this sacred journey. Thank you for being there and for your patience with me. I can be a lulu sometimes, but you already knew that. ☺

I love and honor your presence always, and my Heart will forever remain open to your guidance.

I would like to say a very special thank you to my brother, Danielli, for always being supportive in my life, of my work and always being there for me in every way, unconditionally. You claim to not "really know" what I do. Well, I ask you…why is it you can explain to others what it is you don't understand so well, and get them to understand it? You're a genius…just admit it. ☺ And, thank you for being such an "enlightened" ELF. I couldn't have done my life without you. I love you very much. And to Paulinsky…thank you for putting up with both of us. (tee hee!) I love you too. P.S. I don't believe you read the "small print" on this ELF contract you signed. ☺

To Mom…thank you for putting a deck of Tarot Cards and Edgar Cayce books in my hands when I was twelve years old. Your contract was to remind me of the "Magick". It was a dirty job, but somebody had to do it. (tee hee!) Thanks for listening to the Universe Mom…it was the best thing you ever did for me. I love you.

To Doo Dah…the "Magician" at the Magic Castle, hmmm. Thank you for always being the devil's advocate, always approaching things scientifically, challenging me at every corner and every turn. You helped me to really KNOW who I am in the realm of magick and mysticism, and not to care what anyone thinks, nor to have to go out of my way to prove myself. I know what I know, I see and feel things, and no one can ever change that. You birthed an ancient girlie, so I say to you…thank you for helping me hold my light and to always listen to my Heart. I love you.

To Radi…the light you carry in your soul is beautifully expressed through the extraordinary artwork you've created for this book. Your visions are Divine source itself. I am grateful to you for having been there for me, as this book would not be what it is without you, your compassion and your love. And to Trace…thank you for always being present with your enthusiasm, guidance, brilliant ideas and beautiful thoughts, which have contributed greatly to the development of this book. And, the laughter… ELVES, you can't live with us, and you can't live without us…because we're cute!!! ☺ Vi voglio bene.

To my Bellie Angel Girl…thank you for helping me through the challenges of how to write a book, and put it together. This process would have been next to impossible without your wisdom, and guidance, helping me edit everything from beginning to end. Words cannot really express how grateful I am for all you've done, making this experience very magickal and special, like you. Thank you for being my "Hermetic Angel" and very beautiful soul sister. And a special thank you to Irby and Sofia (my Faery Godchild on the way), for being such a beautiful part of this mystical journey.

Irby, when you sing, your angelic voice is my guide for sound, and is helping me to unfold something greater through my work with the colours and light. Bellie, you are always challenging me to explore my voice. You're nudging me out of my comfort zone just like an Aries, and I love it. And, to baby Sofia… it is, and will always be magickal to watch you sing back to us with love when we surround you in the womb with the frequencies of the colours and the sound of our voices chanting to you. These experiences are so Divine, there are no words. Thank you all for sharing your gorgeous energies with me. I love you.

To Tommy…your role has always been that of an ancient guardian for myself, and my businesses. You've done well in wielding the energies within my sacred temple, and through this journey, tapped into your shaman/warrior nature, remembering the "magick" yourself. Thank you for being an anchor in my life, holding me in when I want to fly, helping me to stay focused. I know it's a challenge sometimes…but then again, you're soul needs challenges to stay "awake". ☺ You truly are a Buddha, and I love you.

To Gina (la weena ☺)… thank you for listening to your Guides and contacting me, at the perfect time, helping me to complete the development of Auracle's Colours. I find it interesting that you had a tattoo of a Heart shaped bottle with spirits coming out, done inside your right arm to the "future" made five years ago that matches exactly in size, the Heart shaped bottles we're using for the colours…hmmm. You were chosen for this, for you are a very gifted and magickal soul. I love you.

To Paul…thank you for everything you've done to help me in so many ways with the development of Auracle's Colour Therapy as a whole. You are a "Buddhaful" soul. Many thanks for all your smiles, laughter and friendship. ☺

To Grandpa…you left this world long ago, yet you have been with me all along. We always had an extraordinary Heart connection, and I still feel it just as strongly as if you were still here with me on the physical plane. You have become an important part of my journey back in time. You are one of my Kings walking me through this literal chapter of my life, and yet I know you walk along side of my very loved friend, Juan. Thank you for joining with another extraordinary soul, making sure I stay on my path. This allows me to do what I love in this world…colour, light, sound…magick. Thank you Grandpa. I love you. P.S. Please say hi to Grandma and give her a big hug.

To Michael…my very special other brother, my Grandfathers real son, and the one person I've known the longest in my life besides my blood family members. Thank you for reminding me when we were children of a lifetime we had together in Egypt many Moons ago. You started me on my path, and continued guiding me throughout the years with all the mystical hours of conversations we had. These journeys with you have accelerated my process and led me to where I am now…and, I believe you knew this was coming. Yet, in your extraordinary silence, I feel your strength and support. Because of this, I will always step off the edge. What a wondrous, whimsical magickal star you are. I love you.

And…a very special Thank You to Juan, a beautiful soul mate, who left this world many years ago. You are always with me and I know this as you make your presence known through one of Alex's favorite bands and album…Pink Floyd/Dark Side of the Moon. Funny how the back cover of this book resembles the pyramid from the Dark Side of the Moon, only it came from Radesha's hands as he designed all Symbols and illustrations in the book. This was your signature Juan, and I know it. Radi has no idea who Pink Floyd is, by the way…hmmm. You told me three years ago to write this book and you were quite adamant about it. You're guidance has accelerated my process by helping me to remember my Hermetic lives…several of which I have shared with you. I know I will see you again, as we are not finished yet. You are my other King. I miss you and will always love you.

And to Alex…if you ever find this book, or it finds you, know I love you, and my Heart will always be connected to you no matter where you are in this world…or out of this world. You are the shadow, the light and a very ancient soul. May your life be as magickal as you are.

To all of you I express once more, I love you with all of my Golden Heart and thank you for coming back to play with me in this "Magickal" sandbox of life. The Universe could not have given me any greater gift.

Table of Contents

Your Beauty is Infinite,

Your Spiritual Heart Divine,

Look deep inside your Magickal Soul,

Who knows what you will find.

Look closely…for it is Love.

What is Auracle's Colour Therapy About?

Auracle's Colour Therapy is about the use of light and colours to help heal disease and illness by bringing physical, emotional, mental and spiritual aspects into complete balance.

Auracle's Colour Therapy is one of the only colour therapy product lines in mister form known worldwide in which all formulations are based on natural ingredients. We do not use substances that are harmful to the users or the environment to keep the frequencies higher, as well as keeping in alignment with the integrity of the company.

The formulations for each colour are carefully chosen. Every Bottle is filled with high frequency oils, gem and flower essences, and archetypal energies to bring to all who use these beautiful jewels the unconditional love of all Angels, Archangels, Masters, Ascended Masters, and Divine realms.

The colours are poured into Heart shaped Bottles because the Heart represents the highest frequency in the world. The mists are available in all colours of the rainbow. The "Royal Set" is composed of Deep Magenta, Red, Coral, Orange, Gold, Yellow, Olive, Green, Turquoise, Blue, Indigo Blue, and Violet with a special blend of Golden sparkles. There is also the "Illumination Set", which includes Pink and Clear, with a special blend of Iridescent sparkles. The Illumination colours are lighter shades representing Universal light shining through for those who wish to release tears and suffering, and allow an accelerated healing to take place. The Illumination colours are also for those who already have a strong connection into Divine realms, wishing to communicate on deeper levels with their guides.

Auracle's Colour Therapy was made with no names or numbers because colour is Universal and does not need to be connected to any outlining system, which tries to define it, therefore narrowing the experience. This allows the soul an opportunity and the power to then experience and create for itself a definition unimposed by boundaries.

How Auracle's Colour Therapy Works

Within light, the full colour spectrum or a "rainbow" can be found. Each colour in the rainbow corresponds to a different part of our anatomy, such as organs, blood, bones, tissues, etc. It is in this manner that colour influences our physical, mental, emotional and spiritual well- being, and has a profound effect on archetypal patterns which rule our lives.

In India, colour has been used for over 5,000 years by diagnosing the "Chakras". Chakra in Sanskrit means "wheel" or "disc". Chakras are energetic bodies of light similar to the Sun and its' rays, sitting within the spinal column of the body branching upward from the base to the crown. Each Chakra, or energy center, has its own specific colour and sound that correlates to different levels of our consciousness.

An aura is an electrical field of energy, which surrounds every living organism. The aura absorbs white light from the atmosphere and divides it into different colour energies. For example, when Newton passed light through a prism, the full spectrum of colours within the light were revealed. Think of our bodies as that prism. Since we are made of light, the colours of Red, Orange, Yellow, Green, Blue, Indigo and Violet are directed into the appropriate Chakras within the physical body to keep it healthy.

The benefits of using colour therapy are infinite and will help accelerate healing with many types of physical ailments, such as cancer, arthritis, back pain, blood disorders, digestive problems and hormonal issues, to name a few. Emotional and mental imbalances can also be healed through colour. The colours can help mend broken Hearts and assist walking through all kinds of fears by gaining self-respect, self-worth, self-love and integrity. The colours can also help shift the energies of judgment and criticism into love and compassion, helping to bring joy and laughter into the Heart again.

An example of a therapeutic technique using colour healing would be the ancient East Indian method of covering a pot of honey with a coloured scarf. In time, the honey would absorb that particular colour once ingested and infuse the appropriate cells of the body needing be healed.

In Traditional Chinese Medicine, each organ of the body is also associated with a specific colour, as well as positive and negative sounds. The body is divided energetically into twelve regions called "meridians". Meridians are like road maps within the body and direct energy into the Lungs, Large Intestine, Stomach, Spleen, Heart, Pericardium (tissue surrounding the Heart), Small Intestine, Bladder, Kidneys, Triple Burner, Gall Bladder and Liver. The life force that fuels these meridians is known as "chi". Through the skin, which is our largest eliminative organ, discoloration can be seen, imbalances within the body can be revealed, and illness diagnosed. Herbs, tinctures and teas containing the proper colours for the organs to be healed would then be prescribed. Through the use of these natural medicines, chi within the meridians would be restored, resulting in a balanced over all health of the spirit, mind and body.

From Ancient History to Modern Technology

Colour therapy has been in existence since Ancient Egypt. It is said the Egyptian priests had solarium style chambers built in their temples with the roofs open and exposed to the Sun. As the Sun passed over the temple, the patients lying in the the chamber would be saturated with healing light. The light would reflect off the different coloured walls, as well as off the various colours of crystals used to line each room to accelerate the healing of a specific medical problem. Unfortunately, there has been little or no physical evidence of that these chambers existed as of yet.

The Egyptian city of Heliopolis, known as the "Greek City of the Sun", was known for its many healing temples which made use of Sunlight separating into spectral components or colours. Again, each component was used to treat a specific medical problem.

These practices were continued throughout Ancient Greece mainly on Kos, better known as the "Island of Medicine". There were 420 temples built in the name of the healing god Aesclepius, in which colour therapies and other healing modalities were used by such masters as Hippocrates and Pythagoras.

The use of colour and light has been continued throughout the ages and is presently being used all over the world. Dr. Peter Mandel, a modern German scientist / acupuncturist /homeopath/ naturopath/ chiropractor has developed a system of acu-light therapy called Esogetic Colorpuncture ™. Coloured light is applied to acupuncture points along meridians to help release blockages and prevent disease. Esogetic Colorpuncture ™ is now being taught worldwide with great success. These treatments and other related therapies can be found in Dr. Mandel's institutions in Germany and Switzerland.

The Purpose of Auracle's Colour Therapy

The purpose of Auracle's Colour Therapy is to connect each soul who uses the Bottles to their higher self, their guides, the Universe and the energy within themselves of God/Goddess/All That Is.

Because the formulations are filled with the energies of many Masters, Ascended Masters, Angels, Archangels, Faeries and other light beings who bring us unconditional love, it allows the Heart to be opened, and will help the seeker to listen to their Heart and align with their true purpose in life without fear or judgment. In order to "hear" our orders from above, we must be open in our Hearts to listen to the truth. It is only then, that the changes in our lives will begin.

When the Bottles are chosen by the seeker, the colours, especially in the order chosen, represent a physical manifestation of the soul's dialogue to itself. This is a story which could explain why the soul came in, its purpose here on earth, its gifts and challenges, possible issues of the moment which need to be dealt with, and how to bring all levels into a perfect state of balance should they pay attention to the message of the Bottles.

This is much like witnessing a symphony composed by the soul manifested through the colours it has chosen. Each colour has a tone, creating chords of the soul's sacred song. This is a song born out of the unspoken, the unconscious, a song which can no longer be hidden or unheard when the light has been introduced, illuminating and penetrating the very depths of the soul.

The colours are here for all to use. We are in an age now where we must take responsibility for healing our diseases to accelerate our health and well–being. Auracle's Colours are magickal keys, here to help us unlock the door to our soul's sacred journey.

Find out what mystical messages lie within your soul. Step off the edge, let go and let God, for the "magick" will happen when you open your Heart.

It is your choice.

How to Use and Begin Readings With Auracle's Colour Therapy Bottles

Using Auracle's Colour Therapy

Auracle's Colour Therapy bottles can be utilized in various ways, assisting in the soul's healing process. This will be explained in further detail below. There is no particular format to use when working with the bottles, as each soul is vastly unique, therefore each person/soul will require different methods of using the colours to reach a higher state of being.

Misting the colours into the auric field (the energy field surrounding the body forming the shape of an egg) is a wonderful way to begin working with the bottles, allowing the frequencies to penetrate the physical, emotional, mental and spiritual layers. This is the first step towards activating the souls transformation.

The bottles may be used in meditation, whether sitting up or lying down. They may be placed on or around the body from the feet to the crown. They may also be placed on all the chakras, or maybe hold a bottle of choice on the Heart chakra, for example.

Other suggestions to accelerate the healing process would be to place a small flashlight over or at the base of the bottle causing the colour or colours chosen to Illuminate. Face the Auracle's Symbol down towards the body, as this will allow quicker penetration into the areas needing to be healed or shifted.

Another suggestion would be to hold the chosen bottle in one hand at least two to three inches above the body, and begin drawing Heart shapes over that area of your body as if the bottle was being used as a pen. As the Heart shape is drawn, the energy of unconditional love immediately enters the body and a deeper shift can occur, often felt by the seeker in the form of a "blissful" feeling inside.

Whatever suggestions there may be, it is still completely up to the seeker as to how to use Auracle's Colour Therapy. There is no incorrect way.

One must always listen to their instincts to see what feels right when working with the bottles. Having fun by trying different methods of working with each bottle is part of the healing process. One may find a particular method that comes quite natural to them. Each of us have an inner sense of soul healing, and once we begin to tap into that part of our highest self, we may find which practice works best with each new moment and situation.

However the bottles are used to experience a Heart awakening and allow the energy of love and light to flow through the body is the right way to do it. This energy flow will allow the healing to take place on all levels.

How to Read the Colours Chosen

We all have a "Soul Colour", meaning there may be one or possibly a few colours we've gravitated towards all of our lives. The soul colour will generally tell us why we are here, about our personality, our challenges, our life purpose and or Hearts desire. One must not only see the positives within the colours chosen, but also embrace the negatives in order to learn, to grow, and to push ourselves beyond the "box".

If it is a **life reading** (information showing progression of life purpose from birth to present time), the soul colour or colours will most likely continue to re-occur in other readings. If the reading is reflective of a **present happening** (an immediate issue), they may not. It is very important to pay attention to the order in which the bottles are chosen.

Choosing Bottles One, Two and Three

Bottle One represents the left wing of the seeker, **Bottle Two** represents the body of the seeker, and **Bottle Three** represents the right wing of the seeker. In essence, one will see the image of an Angelic presence when arranging the two wings behind the body of the chosen bottles.

The left and right wings (Bottles One and Three) represent the archetypal energies (Wizard, Priestess, Healer, Victim, Warrior, Artist, Leader, Mystic, Teacher, Scientist, etc.), which are the driving forces behind our soul fulfilling its path, or present situation being worked with.

The body (Bottle Two) represents challenges of issues lifelong and/ or present, and how these challenges are manifesting themselves in the physical world to possibly create suffering. Together all three bottles reveal the souls challenges, destiny and purpose of its incarnation in this life.

Note from the Author:

By choosing Auracle's Colour Therapy, we are literally choosing what is in our Hearts, as the bottles are Heart shaped. The colours we choose are our personal messages from our higher selves and our guides coming through that we must pay attention to in order to stay balanced and experience love and joy in this world.

The significance of the three bottles is to remind us of our true Angelic or "light" nature. NONE of us are born into damnation from which we cannot ascend. If we are made in Gods image, this would insinuate God was damned as well. Does this really feel right to any of us? No. If you listen to your Heart, that concept will not resonate as true or truth. What is true is we are born of love and light as children of this Universe, and we have all possibilities of doing anything and everything we wish. As light beings we have the choice of taking the higher paths, radiating our light into the world and to those around us. If we choose to think of ourselves as damned, we keep ourselves in darkness and continue to suffer.

The first step in changing our consciousness is to recognize that holding on to an old way of thinking which isn't helping us heal must be shifted. As the Masters say, "If the energy isn't right, turn around and walk the other way". This means let go of that which no longer serves us.

We must be able to see ourselves through the eyes of an unconditional Heart, our Heart. Yet, it is most important we forgive ourselves for thinking we were anything less than loving, beautiful and precious. It is also important to forgive those who unknowingly made us feel this way.

Forgiveness is the magical key. By choosing forgiveness, we WILL bring more love into this world, and most importantly, back into our own Hearts.

The Illumination Bottles

A note to the reader

In the "Descriptions of Auracle's Colour Therapy Bottles" you will find all "Royal" colours with their descriptions. The two exceptions are the Illuminated Red (Pink) Bottle, and the Clear Bottle because they represent the completion of the entire spectrum of colours.

All descriptions of the Royal Bottles apply to the Illumination Bottles except they signify the "Harmonious and Dysfunctional" energies **intensified**. For instance, if one were to choose the Royal Orange Bottle, of the many positive scenarios that might be possible, one scenario might speak to them of moving into a cycle of creation, such as developing a new project, wanting to paint the house or change the furniture, even ideas of re- birthing oneself or a new baby. Orange can also represent the awakening of one's sensuality, and nurturing energies for the self and others. If the Illumination Orange Bottle were chosen, it might signify that the person is already in the accelerated state of what is being created or re-birthed, by listening to guidance from within, and higher realms. Orange in the positive also represents having the courage to do what one is being moved to do, no matter how ridiculous it seems to others.

If one were to choose the Royal Orange Bottle, of the many negative scenarios that might be possible, one scenario might speak to them of an addiction or trauma, whether it is smoking, drugs, coffee, sugar, or emotional, mental or physical abuse which needs to be acknowledged and healed to prevent health problems further down the road. However, given the same scenario with Illumination Orange Bottle, it would signify that the soul can no longer stay in the same position of housing and feeding into the addiction or trauma. These issue/issues have already caused immense toxicity, suffering and illness within the body creating medical problems because it has gone on for so long and been ignored.

The Illumination Bottles will be chosen by the seeker when an accelerated level of awakening begins. Whether it is because of intense suffering the soul can no longer handle, or simply that the seeker choosing the Bottles already has a extraordinary connection to the Divine, possibly being in the healing profession, for instance…it is still saying to the soul that it must move quickly, and remain at "Light"ening speed to complete their process being guided from above.

Illumination is what happens when there is a willingness of the Ka (Egyptian word for soul) to surrender, opening up to dialogue with the Divine realms such as Angels, Archangels, Masters and other Light Beings who are here to help us serve our higher purpose in this world.

The Illumination Bottles represent the "light" of God/Goddess/All That Is shining through the darker, denser energies, exposing issues of present and or past to be worked through immediately. In this aspect, the Illumination Bottles signify that the soul can no longer stay in its present position of suffering, but instead must accelerate to bring in a newer energy and a higher frequency within.

It is by listening to our inner wisdom, our voice, as well as those from above in which our inner illumination occurs, that allows us to walk our path with light.

Caring For Your Auracle's Colour Therapy Bottles

Auracle's Colour Therapy Bottles are developed through energies of light, so it is not recommended to keep the Bottles in a box, in dark areas, or simply hidden away. Auracle's Colour Bottles should be displayed in the openness of a room, on glass shelves, an altar, or even be carried around by the owner of the Bottles as often as possible, keeping the Bottles close to the Heart or body. By keeping the Bottles close to you, experiences of more loving energies and protection will be present in all situations. You are more likely to remember the guidance and love that constantly surrounds you by having the Bottles interacting with you in your daily lives.

Because the Bottles carry energies of the Divine, they should not be put on the floor, with the exceptions of self-healing by the seeker, or in professional treatments only. It is recommended to place the Bottles for display in the home, office, or anywhere from the waist up, if possible.

It is also important to remember since all colours are filled with an abundance of light, they should not be stored in direct Sunlight, nor should be exposed for any length of time in temperatures above 80-85°.

All of Auracle's Colours wish to be in the open to interact with those who have chosen them to bring in that which we all need most… healing of the Heart.

Note to the Reader: Recommended flashlights to use during personal or professional treatments with Auracle's Colour Therapy are Coast LED's.

Illustration of Body Chakras

BODY CHAKRAS

© 2006 Auracle's Colour Therapy

Descriptions of

Auracle's Colour Therapy

Bottles

Royal Magenta Bottle

Other Names: First Chakra or Eighth Chakra (depending upon belief system)

Location: The Root or above the Crown area

Colour: Magenta

Element: Cosmic Energy

Opposite Colour: Olive

Gems/Minerals: Magenta Fluorite, Hematite, Ruby, Holdenite, Black Opal

Symbolism: Angels

Archetypes: The Caretakers' caretaker/Universal healer, Angel (Functional), Fallen Angel (Dysfunctional)

Area of Consciousness: Ketheric Body (where we merge with God and "All That Is")

Governs: Our connection to Angels and Divine realms

Physical Attributes: Hormonal system, reproductive organs, eyes, head.

Harmonious Energy: Compassion, (Divine) love, detachment, (infinite) intelligence, tenderness, protection, passion, concentration, energetic, love of the little things in life, in service of others, deep sense of spirituality, sees the Divine in all things.

Dysfunctional Energy: Spiritual disillusionment, depression (not receiving "enough" love from others), feels that life is too hard, overexertion, overwork, feels unsafe.

Illness: Deafness, dis-ease.

Using Your Royal and Illumination Magenta Bottles: When using Auracle's Colours, always face the Symbol on the Bottles towards your body. Shake the Bottles thoroughly, and spray the energies around the body from head to toe. Breathe deeply, inhaling the beautiful aromas of Magenta. Place the Bottles on your Root or Crown Chakras, or wherever they feel best on or around your body. To accelerate the healing and intensify the saturation of the Magenta frequencies place a small flashlight at the base or behind each Bottle, causing the colours to illuminate. Auracle's Colours may be left on the body for any length of time desired, accompanied by any other colours of choice. However, it is not recommended or necessary to saturate your energy field with the colours for more than 20-30 minutes at a time **if using flashlights**. Conscious shifts may occur immediately depending on the level of healing called in by the soul. All experiences are unique.

Reflections of Balance Through Meditation: While sitting or lying down, place the

Bottle/Bottles on or around your body, as directed above. Close your eyes and become aware of the Auracle's Symbol, focusing on the Heart in the center of the Symbol, with the Magenta, Pink, White and Golden rays extending into all of your Chakras like the Sun. The more deeply you allow yourself to feel these beautiful energies nurturing your very being, the more TRUST and LOVE you will feel for yourself and others in this world. When we feel the light and energy of trust moving through our being it is easier to "Let Go, and Let God", and to feel safe with how the Universe is moving us to keep us on our path.

Keynote: Divine love is the GREATER LOVE of God/Goddess/All That Is. It is our ability to receive love and give love back to all sentient beings without hidden agendas, judgment or attachments, but simply with compassion and unconditional love. It is this Divine love that opens up the soul and sings to our human spirit.

Royal Red Bottle

Other Names: First Chakra, Root Chakra, Base Chakra, Muladhara, Kundalini Center (Sanskrit)

Location: Base of the spine or tailbone (point between the anus and sex organs)

Colour: Red or Red/Magenta

Verb: I have

Sense: Smell

Element: Earth

Opposite Colour: Green

Gems/Minerals: Red Diamond, Red Garnet, Red Tourmaline, and Bloodstone

Symbolism: Snakes and Dragons (historically representing Kundalini fire energy), the cleansing flame of the Holy Spirit and the rising of the Phoenix from the ashes.

Archetypes: Mother (Functional), Prostitute, Victim, Energetic Vampire (Dysfunctional)

Area of Consciousness: Physical Body

Governs: Willpower and how we see ourselves; Our perceptions in the physical world.

Physical Attributes: Skeletal structure (spine and bones), cellular structure, lymphatic system, blood, adrenals, bladder and kidneys (elimination system), menstrual cycle, conception and birth, legs, ankles, and feet.

Harmonious Energy: Love, life force, enthusiasm, being present in the "here and now", success, unlimited physical energy, passion, drive, earthly pleasure, manifestation of material abundance, solidity, survival instincts, sense of grounding, being centered, willpower, determination, stability and detachment.

Dysfunctional Energy: Survival issues, control issues, problems with the Mother, frigidity, anger, rage, sexual issues, domineering, chaotic, sense of being ungrounded (disconnection to Mother Earth), lack of ability to manifest abundance, feelings of being unlovable and lost.

Illness: High blood pressure, Heart attack, anemia, cancer, gynecological problems, fever, swelling and adrenal exhaustion.

Using Your Royal Red Bottle: When using Auracle's Colours, always face the Symbol on the Bottle towards your body. Shake the Bottle thoroughly, and spray the energies around the body from head to toe. Breathe deeply, inhaling the beautiful aromas of

Red. Place the Bottle between your feet, legs, Root and or Heart Chakras, or wherever it feels best on or around your body. To accelerate the healing and intensify the saturation of the Red frequency, place a small flashlight at the base or behind the Bottle, causing the colour to illuminate. Auracle's Colours may be left on the body for any length of time desired, accompanied by any other colours of choice. It is not recommended or necessary to saturate your energy field with the colours for more than 20-30 minutes at a time **if using flashlights**. Conscious shifts may occur immediately depending on the level of healing called in by the soul. All experiences are unique.

Reflections of Balance Through Meditation: While sitting or lying down, place the Bottle on or around your body as directed above. Close your eyes and begin to feel the heat coming from the illuminating Red light as if flames are shooting from the Earth into your feet, up your legs, torso, chest, neck, and up through your Crown Chakra, and back down into the Earth again. Let this cycle of Red energy continue to move through your body and into the Earth until you feel completely connected and grounded. It is normal to feel a warm sensation as your body is heating up through the Red frequency.

Keynote: Because the Root Chakra pertains to the Physical body itself, any "physical" discipline would be wonderful. Activities such as dancing, walking, running, swimming, martial arts, massage, yoga and aerobics will help unleash the Kundalini for passionate energy as well as helping to bring in the feelings of strength, grounding and being present in the "here and now". Red also signifies the "awakening" of the soul. In essence, Red is here to help us feel safe in walking the earth, stay present and conscious with all we do, and love being here in the bodies we have chosen.

* Caution: If you have HIGH BLOOD PRESSURE or HEART PROBLEMS, do not attempt this meditation as it may aggravate your present situation. You may want to consider working with the Illumination Red (Pink) Bottle and its recommended meditation as it contains a softer energy.

Royal Coral Bottle

Other Names: None

Location: Between the Root and Sacral Chakras

Colour: Coral

Element: Earth/Water

Opposite Colour: Turquoise

Gems/Minerals: Coral, Rose Quartz, Carnelian, Topaz, Opal

Symbolism: The great Coral reefs found in the Mediterranean, Australian and South Pacific Oceans and seas.

Archetypes: Philanthropist (Functional), Convict/Martyr (Dysfunctional)

Area of Consciousness: Physical Body

Governs: Our compassion and spiritual connection to the communities around us, to all sentient beings, and to the world itself.

Physical Attributes: Skeletal structure, digestive system, sexual organs

Harmonious Energy: Understands and aligns with the "New Christ Ray" (having shifted from the Piscean Age of sacrifice to the Aquarian Age of taking responsibility for one's actions). Knows how to impart deep wisdom to others through loving words, is aware of the process of rebirth within oneself and in others, enjoys counseling, embraces new technology without difficulty, loves beauty and creating beautiful environments in which to live and work, is aesthetic, loyal, courageous, generous, benevolent, interdependent, emotionally sensitive to others, has the ability to protect others by understanding boundaries and holding "sacred space," enjoys doing community service as it is working for the greater whole of humanity, embraces the awakening of love for the self, thereby bringing in the possibilities of experiencing enlightenment/bliss.

Dysfunctional Energy: Extreme shock and trauma (including that of birth), emotionally high strung and explosive, repeatedly enters relationships and experiences unrequited love (a love not being returned), has experienced all types of abuses (physical, mental, emotional), broken promises, has no boundaries and feels vulnerable because of this, has feelings of aloneness instead of ALL-ONE-NESS, projects positives and negatives onto others instead of taking responsibility for their actions, dependency, co-dependency, attached to old thought forms and patterns that no longer serve the soul, has issues with abandonment, competitiveness and a broken Heart, survival, inability to embrace love of the self.

Illness: Digestive and circulation problems, adrenal burnout, psychosomatic illnesses.

Using Your Royal and Illumination Coral Bottles: When using Auracle's Colours, always face the Symbol on the Bottles towards your body. Shake the Bottles thoroughly, and spray the energies around the body from head to toe. Breathe deeply, inhaling the beautiful aromas of Coral. Place the Bottles on your Sacral or Heart Chakras, or wherever they feel best on or around your body. To accelerate the healing and intensify the saturation of the Coral frequencies, place a small flashlight at the base or behind each Bottle, causing the colours to illuminate. Auracle's Colours may be left on the body for any length of time desired, accompanied by any other colours of choice. It is not recommended or necessary to saturate your energy field with the colours for more than 20-30 minutes at a time **if using flashlights**. Conscious shifts may occur immediately depending on the level of healing called in by the soul. All experiences are unique.

Reflections of Balance Through Meditation: While sitting or lying down, place the Bottle/Bottles on or around your body as directed above. Close your eyes and feel the Coral light radiating into every cell of your body, allowing the Coral frequency to penetrate still further, into your skeletal structure. Visualize your entire being glowing with Coral light. Let this energy fill your Heart with unconditional love and nurture your soul. As you are feeling this beautiful colour saturating your body, ask how you can bring more love, compassion and forgiveness into yourself. Your Guides are only dimensions away. They will answer through your Heart. Just listen. The more you experience the Coral light, the more love and compassion you will feel for yourself and will begin to forgive yourself and others more easily. This will radiate from your entire being into the world, and because of this, you will receive more "requited" and nurturing love from others. The Coral ray will help to fill the emptiness in your Heart, and in your life. During this meditation, feel the joy radiating from every cell as you allow the Coral light to saturate your soul.

Keynote: Coral is the "New Christ Ray" which is shifting our consciousness to take responsibility upon ourselves, for our choices and our very lives. Christ's teachings were about following our own Hearts, our sacred Hearts in which we have a direct line to God and all Angels, Archangels, Faeries, Masters and so on who work with us. If we listen to our Hearts, we will always do the right thing.

However, what if the right thing for you doesn't seem right to anyone else when you voice it? Would you then give up your guidance and continue living in a way that is depressing you or even making you sick? Would you give up your dreams because of what another says to you out of their own fears? Do you have the courage to step out and go where nobody else dares to go for fear of judgment?

The Coral ray is about being able to detach from other thought forms that are not right for you with Divine love at your side. It is about having the courage to stand up for yourself in a family, or in a relationship/marriage, which abuses you or is abusive to others, or standing up to a community living in a manner you do not wish to live in because it is no longer serving you. It is about having the courage to think for yourself and push your own boundaries, and about going out on a limb and taking a leap of "FAITH" to trust your guidance and not have to get anyone else's opinion on something they are not qualified to judge. It is your life, no one else's, so who are you living it for?

To bring in the Coral ray ask yourself where in your life are you being betrayed, or better yet…how are you betraying yourself? What in your life must change in order to bring you peace and bring you into a more loving place?

Is it your career, your relationship, your home or family? Listen very carefully, for your Guides are always speaking to you. Just be ready for what they have to say and follow it. The more steps you take to listen and be open for the changes you need to occur in your life, the more gifts the Universe will bestow upon you because you are taking responsibility to help yourself.

Loving and having compassion for ourselves and others is the greatest gift of all, for wasn't this the greatest teaching of Christ? Could this in fact be what is meant by the "Second coming of Christ"…not the physical aspect of the man coming forth to save us, but saving ourselves through the awakening of our own Hearts?

Remember, Coral grows in the sea, thus it is associated with unconscious and subconscious energies. The little animals within the Corals' constitution sacrifice their individuality to become "joined" with others as a part of the whole for the greater good of the community. Because the Coral reefs need light to grow, they always strive for the "light." A reminder to us that the Coral is symbolic of the skeletal structure, and if the reef is poisoned its structure will crumble and die. We are as fragile. Like Coral, our journey as beings is to move towards and into the light. It is to experience the awakening of the spiritual self…to love ourselves, to be loved and to receive love with open arms and an open Heart. It is here that our higher intuition speaks to us so that we embrace our ability to detach from all things that no longer serve us, and call to our very being the experience of enlightenment, bliss, and nirvana, should we listen.

Royal Orange Bottle

Other Names: Sacral Chakra, Spleen Chakra, Svadhisthana (Sanskrit)

Location: Center of the Abdomen, 1-2 inches below the belly button

Colour: Orange

Verb: I feel

Sense: Taste

Element: Water

Opposite Colour: Blue

Gems/Minerals: Carnelian, Orange Diamond, Orange Tourmaline, Ruby, Opal, Herkimer Diamond

Symbolism: Orange robes of Tibetan Monks and Hindi gurus, at one with the "wholeness" of the Universe and All That Is/Renunciation, the Orange tree…evergreen and ever-bearing/fruitfulness.

Archetypes: Empress/Emperor, Lover/Seducer, Pioneer, (Functional), Martyr/Addict/Prisoner (Dysfunctional).

Area of Consciousness: Emotions

Governs: Creativity, feelings of sexuality and sensuality, clairsentience (the ability to "feel" what is unseen by the naked eye.)

Physical Attributes: Kidneys, ovaries, testicles, prostate, spleen, mammary glands.

Harmonious Energy: Nurturing, sensuality (sexuality for pleasure and joy), bliss, gregariousness, creativity, a higher sense of humor, intuition (gut feelings), the ability to master sociability, ones emotions, trust, healthy appetite, deep insights, interdependence, enlightenment, pleasure, devotion, desire, healthy sense of belonging, close relationships, warmth and compassion, ecstasy, ability to detach.

Dysfunctional Energy: Abuse of all kinds (Physical, mental, emotional), addictions, dependency, co-dependency, sacrificial (martyr), shock, trauma, betrayal, suffering, emotionally explosive, hysteria, overindulgence, reproductive and sexual disorders, manipulation.

Illness: Thyroid, muscle cramps, kidney weakness, constipation, sterility, nerve pain, eating disorders (loss of weight and obesity).

Using Your Royal and Illumination Orange Bottles: When using Auracle's Colours, always face the Symbol on the Bottles towards your body. Shake the Bottles thoroughly, and spray the energies around the body from head to toe. Breathe deeply, inhaling the beautiful aromas of Orange. Place the Bottles on your Sacral Chakra, two inches below the belly button, over the ovaries or prostate areas, or wherever they feel best on or around your body. To accelerate the healing and intensify the saturation of the Orange frequencies, place a small flashlight at the base or behind each Bottle, causing the colours to illuminate. Auracle's Colours may be left on the body for any length of time desired, accompanied by any other colours of choice. It is not recommended or necessary to saturate your energy field with the colours for more than 20-30 minutes at a time **if using flashlights**. Conscious shifts may occur immediately depending on the level of healing called in by the soul. All experiences are unique.

<u>**Reflections of Balance Through Meditation:**</u> While sitting or lying down, place the Bottles on or around your body as directed above. Close your eyes and visualize a bright Orange Sun bursting out from the inside the Sacral area. Feel the warmth, nurturing and sensual energies of the Orange light moving through the ovaries and prostate. Let this light continue to saturate these areas, and allow the energy to move through to other areas of the body as well including the Heart. Allowing this, you may experience an emotional release, which is quite normal, and will help to boost the immune system of the Sacral Chakra. As the Orange frequencies penetrate your energy field, the more nurturing will be felt, thus bringing more love into the body, balancing the emotions if a shock or trauma has been experienced.

<u>**Keynote:**</u> Because the Sacral Chakra pertains to our reproductive area for birthing and creation, belly dancing of all types would be a wonderful and fun way to "unlock" the Sacral or hip area. This will allow the energy to circulate freely, to awaken one's sensuality and desires.

Another important factor which most people have a difficult time with is detachment. It is most important to "cut" the chains of the past in order for the soul to accelerate on any level. To live in the past is to condemn one's soul, stealing its vital and creative energy needed to move forward. When we live in the past, the chains we forge begin to slowly eat away not only at our soul, but also within our biological tissue. This can and will cause illness.

Once enough energy has been borrowed over and over from the body and there is none left for oneself, then the neediness begins. Thus, we will experience the "energetic vampire". At one time or another most people have experienced being around someone who left them feeling completely drained and didn't know why at first. This is the person who now seeks to pull energy from others because they used their supply up by constantly living in the past.

We have no foothold in either the past or the future. Living within those "illusions" is a waste of valuable time and energy. Our power lies in the "here and now". We must always be mindful of this and honor our spirits true journey by letting go of what no longer serves us, even if it means walking away from people, places or things we are used to. Do you have the courage to walk through the wall of fire, or will you stand in front of it and melt? It is your choice.

Remember, "detachment" is the key, for all meetings end in partings and all buildings end in ruin…so the yogis say.

Royal Gold Bottle

Other Names: None

Location: Between the Sacral and Solar Plexus Chakras.

Colour: Gold

Element: Water/Fire

Opposite Colour: Indigo

Gems/Minerals: Topaz, Citrine

Symbolism: The Holy Grail (something attained with great difficulty), the Golden Egg (representing the "wholeness" of the soul), the wise owl, the Golden wedding ring (a Symbol of unity), the lion (strength).

Archetypes: King (Midas), Healer, Saint, Judge, Scribe, Master/Spiritual Teacher (Functional), Miser, False Healer, Thief (Dysfunctional)

Area of Consciousness: Mental and Emotional Body

Governs: Our ability to assimilate life and connections to our deepest fears and inner wisdom.

Physical Attributes: Skin, kidney, nerves, spine and intestines.

Harmonious Energy: Inner wisdom, healer, courage, will power, humor, justice, purity, beauty, trusts gut instincts, benevolence, generosity, manifests material and spiritual wealth, discernment, clarity, mental alertness, independence, warmth, being conscious of right and wrong, easily makes decisions, spiritual wisdom.

Dysfunctional Energy: Deep fears and confusion, anxiety, greed, nervousness, deception, false modesty, self-righteousness, cowardice, false healer, false wizard, cheater, indecisive, misuse of power, bitterness, disgust for self.

Illness: Skin and intestinal disorders, kidney problems, all types of addictions.

Using Your Royal and Illumination Gold Bottles: When using Auracle's Colours, always face the Symbol on the Bottles towards your body. Shake the Bottles thoroughly, and spray the energies around the body from head to toe. Breathe deeply, inhaling the beautiful aromas of Gold. Place the Bottles on your Solar Plexus, Heart Chakra, or wherever they feel best on or around your body. To accelerate the healing and intensify the saturation of the Gold frequencies, place a small flashlight at the base or behind each Bottle, causing the colours to illuminate. Auracle's Colours may be left on the body for any length of time desired, accompanied by any other colours of choice. It is not recommended or necessary to saturate your energy field with the colours for more than

20-30 minutes at a time **if using flashlights**. Conscious shifts may occur immediately depending on the level of healing called in by the soul. All experiences are unique.

<u>Reflections of Balance Through Meditation:</u> While sitting or lying down, place the Bottle/Bottles on or around your body as directed above. Close your eyes and visualize two Angels above your left and right shoulders. Each has a chalice filled with liquid Gold "light". As they begin to pour this Golden light from the chalices above your Crown, feel its warming sensation melt over your entire body weaving its way down from your Crown and all of your Chakras. Feel this slowly moving through your blood stream, your cells, your muscles, your bones, down to your toes. It should feel as if you have submerged yourself under the most beautiful Golden waterfall with water as warm as the Mediterranean Sea flowing endlessly over your body. Let the warmth of the Golden light penetrate every part of your being. Feel this energy radiating out like the Sun, from where the Gold Bottles sit on your body. Now, feel the power of this light radiating from every Chakra. After a while, you will feel the Gold light bursting from every cell of your body.

<u>Keynote:</u> Gold is the alchemy of the soul. It is our souls search for the Holy Grail, for our Golden light within…our "Heart of Gold", if you will. King Arthur's journey was much the same as he searched for the wholeness and peace within. It was a journey that only he could take because it was his soul he had to retrieve. When the King fell apart, so did the land and it's people because the King was the land and the land was the King. So, when King Arthur was in harmony and centered within his own being…listening to the truth of his Heart, the land of Camelot and its people were at peace and all was well.

Spiritual wisdom is earned by honoring our Hearts, by doing things which are loving for our souls. Our self-esteem will naturally grow with every gesture we make by listening to and following through with decisions that open up our Hearts and make us feel good. We all know when something doesn't feel right…listen to that voice, that feeling and let it guide you into a different direction. This is ultimately about how much you are willing trust your guidance from the Universe, God/Goddess/All That Is.

Love can give us the courage to take a "leap of faith" into the unknown, to push our boundaries where we've not journeyed before. Faith does not exist in temples or churches, which are simply empty buildings with beautiful art. FAITH exists in our Hearts. If we have faith, we can carry it wherever we go, including temples and churches. Simply request help to from the Universe and your Guides, then sit quietly and listen for the answers…they will come, maybe not right away and most likely not in linear form, but they will come. As you read this, your Guides are speaking to you…

Do you have the courage to listen?

Royal Yellow Bottle

Other Names: Solar Plexus, Power Center, Manipura (Sanskrit).

Location: The "V" formed by the ribcage above the belly button.

Colour: Yellow or Yellow/Gold

Verb: I can

Sense: Sight

Element: Fire

Opposite Colour: Violet

Gems/Minerals: Yellow Diamond, Yellow Tourmaline, Yellow Sapphire

Symbolism: The warmth, beauty and happiness of the Sun, the Sunflower that always "follows the light."

Archetypes: Warrior/Scholar/Teacher/Hero (Functional), Servant/ Slave (Dysfunctional)

Area of Consciousness: Mental body.

Governs: Emotions dealing with personal power.

Physical Attributes: Kidneys, pancreas, liver, skin, diaphragm, digestive organs, stomach, large intestine.

Harmonious Energy: Laughter, joy, humor, childlike, confidence, intelligence, mental activity, good boundaries, bravery, personal power, willpower, warmth, generosity, self-respect, self-worth, self-esteem, self-love, self-discipline, justice, honor, integrity, playfulness, manifest goals.

Dysfunctional Energy: Too much "in the head", fear, criticism, judgment, cowardess (yellow- bellied), nervousness, lack of confidence, confusion, egocentric, worry, feeling powerless, lack of self-worth, self-love and self-esteem, rejection, feeling unworthy, separation, doubt, anxiety, cynicism, indecisiveness, having no boundaries.

Illness: Digestive difficulties, bloating, liver dysfunction, adrenal dysfunction, food allergies, gallstones, skin disorders, diabetes.

Using Your Royal and Illumination Yellow Bottles: When using Auracle's Colours, always face the Symbol on the Bottle towards your body. Shake the Bottles thoroughly, and spray the energies around the body from head to toe. Breathe deeply, inhaling the beautiful aroma of Yellow. Place the Bottles on your Solar Plexus anywhere from your belly button up to the sternum, or wherever they feel best on or around your body. If you are experiencing extreme fear or digestive problems, you can connect the Bottles, one above the other, up the center of your body like your spine. To accelerate the healing and intensify the saturation of the Yellow frequencies, place a small flashlight at the base or behind each Bottle causing the colours to illuminate. Auracle's Colours may be left on the body for any length of time desired, accompanied by any other colours of choice. It is not recommended or necessary to saturate your energy field with the colours for more than 20-30 minutes at a time **if using flashlights**. Conscious shifts may occur immediately depending on the level of healing called in by the soul. All experiences are unique.

<u>**Reflections for Balance Through Meditation:**</u> While sitting or lying down, place the Bottle/Bottles on or around your body as directed above. Close your eyes and visualize the Auracle's Colour Therapy Symbol in the center of your Solar Plexus and Heart Chakras, and see Yellow rays shooting out of both areas as if you were watching the Suns rays bursting out of your body. Feel the warmth of the energies in the Bottles, and love and light penetrating your entire being. It is not unusual when experiencing the Yellow light moving through your body to feel bliss/euphoria and joy.

<u>**Keynote:**</u> To judge is to limit ourselves, and everything around us, so bring in the intentions of living with more tolerance and acceptance towards all sentient beings. To be in the moment is the greatest way to stand in our power. When we laugh we feel "light"…and where there is light, there is love.

By choosing Yellow, our souls and the Universe are saying it's time to "cut cords" with all unhealthy people, situations and unworthy dietary habits which cause us to suffer needlessly. We must hold integrity within our souls, and continuously reverberate this into the world and to everyone we meet. The Yellow calls upon the halos of Angels, Archangels, Masters and Ascended Masters in which we can better see our true light and feel the love within our being as they reflect this to us. However, we must allow them in.

There is the old saying…"Let go, Let God". This is one of the greatest of Universal truths, and carries the power to change your life forever. Another old saying is… "Laughter is the Best Medicine". Therefore, another suggestion would be to watch funny movies and place either or both Yellow Bottles on your tummy (Solar Plexus) and laugh until you are about to bust!

Remember, Yellow is the colour of joy, but it is also the colour of the "Spiritual Warrior" who fights for their spiritual independence. So, be brave and step off the edge. Give yourself a reason to celebrate your life. What are you waiting for?

Royal Olive Bottle

Other Names: None

Location: Between the Solar Plexus and the Heart Chakras

Colour: Olive

Element: Fire/Air

Opposite Colour: Magenta

Gems/Minerals: Moldevite, Emerald, Yellow Diamond, Opal, Herkimer Diamond

Symbolism: The dove with the olive branch in its beak offering a message of peace and hope to Noah after the flood, the gift given to Ancient Greece (now known as Athens) by Athena of the Olive Tree from which the oils produce "light."

Archetypes: Leader/Giver (Functional), Follower/Trickster (Dysfunctional)

Area of Consciousness: Mental and Astral Body

Governs: The Heart awakening. Surrendering our Will to the truth of our Hearts, becoming empowered.

Physical Attributes: Heart, lungs, gall bladder, large intestine

Harmonious Energy: Leadership qualities, clarity on the path, ability to transform the spiritual into daily life (could be a spiritual counselor), self-love, detachment from one's own emotions, thereby allowing wise decisions to be made from the Heart, and in doing so, shows vulnerability as well as strength, brings hope and joy to self and others through wisdom and laughter, lives in truth, possesses humorously "mischievous" qualities (as would an elf or leprechaun in Celtic lore), in harmony with life, optimistic, deeply connected to nature.

Dysfunctional Energy: Disempowerment; harbors bitterness; rigid; lacks joy; is critical of self and others; may feel envy and jealousy toward others more fortunate, ungrounded, listens to "rationalization" of the mind rather than the truth from the Heart…therefore could be "off" the path; fearful of expressing feelings, spacey, pessimistic, disconnected to Mother Earth.

Illness: Problems with the chest area, large intestine (diarrhea) and cramps.

Using Your Royal and Illumination Olive Bottles: When using Auracle's Colours, always face the Symbol on the Bottles towards your body. Shake the Bottle thoroughly, and spray the energies around the body from head to toe. Breathe deeply, inhaling the beautiful aromas of Olive. Place the Bottles around the sternum of Heart areas, or wherever they feel best on or around your body. To accelerate the healing and intensify the Olive Frequencies, place a small flashlight at the base or behind the Bottle, causing the colour to illuminate. Auracle's Colours may be left on the body for any length of time desired, accompanied by any other colours of choice. It is not recommended or necessary to saturate your energy field with the colours for more than 20-30 minutes at a time **if using flashlights**. Conscious shifts may occur immediately depending on the level of healing called in by the soul. All experiences are unique.

Reflections of Balance Through Meditation: While sitting or lying down, place the Bottle/Bottles on or around your body as directed above. Close your eyes and let the Olive frequency penetrate into your Solar Plexus and Heart Chakras. Visualize the words "Truth" and "Wisdom" being placed into your upper spine, aligning with these Chakras. As the Olive energies penetrate deeper into your being, visualize the Olive light bursting out of your Heart Chakra like an explosion of light moving out to the Universe. As you do this, you may experience feelings of joy, and the more you experience the Olive light, the more you will feel empowerment and strength filling your Heart.

Keynote: Empowerment can be achieved simply by consciously working day by day, living with integrity and being honorable to the self and others. Examples would be holding one's own word by keeping promises made; showing up on time (wherever it may be); be kind to others versus judgmental (remembering to walk a mile in their shoes first); making conscious decisions to benefit ones' health and mental state of being by eating healthier foods to strengthen the body and honor it as a sacred temple, by working out (yoga/pilates) to help strengthen the Solar Plexus, and any type of loving meditation to benefit ones' emotions and expand spiritual awareness.

All of these aspects can help to strengthen ones' being and will bring in higher levels of self-love, self-acceptance, self-esteem, self-worth, self-confidence, and self-respect. Always listen to the Heart, for it is the center of truth and will never lie to you. It is within the qualities of honor, integrity and an open Heart, that the leader can be found, and joy can be expressed. When your Heart and Solar Plexus are congruent, you are indeed on your Divine path.

Royal Green Bottle

Other Names: Heart Chakra, Anahata (Sanskrit)

Location: Center of the Chest

Colour: Emerald Green, (Pink or Gold representing higher dimensions of the Heart)

Verb: I love

Sense: Touch

Element: Air

Opposite Colour: Red

Gems/Minerals: Emerald, Jade, Green Tanzanite, Green Diamond, Herkimer Diamond

Symbolism: Nature's spirits (Faeries, Elves, Pan, the Green Man), the "Seeker" of truth and love.

Archetypes: The Lover (Pan), the Benefactor, (Functional), Actor/Actress, Lucifer, The Fallen Angel (Dysfunctional).

Area of Consciousness: Astral body

Governs: Love (unconditional love), compassion

Physical Attributes: Heart, lungs, blood, lymph glands, circulatory system, endocrine system (hormones), thymus gland (immune system)

Harmonious Energy: Loving relationships of all types, the ability to love, truth, compassion, forgiveness, hope, self-realization, balance, openness, love of nature, ability to give and receive, ability to heal the self and others, decisiveness, intimacy, inspirational, diplomatic, trusting, open to change, connection to all things (oneness), awareness of justice, empathy for humankind, ability to transcend the limitations of life.

Dysfunctional Energy: Terrified of rejection, disillusionment, moodiness, betrayal, jealousy, envy, unable to forgive or have compassion, vulnerability, deception, indecisiveness, excessive behavior to cover up pain of the Heart, feeling constricted, standing at the crossroads of life, inability to allow change in one's life, feeling sorry for oneself, feeling unworthy of love.

Illness: Heart attack, high blood pressure, Heart pain, asthma, insomnia, paranoia, fatigue, negativity, disorders of the immune system, claustrophobia.

Using Your Royal and Illumination Green Bottles: When using Auracle's Colours, always face the Symbol on the Bottles towards your body. Shake the Bottles thoroughly, and spray the energies around the body from head to toe. Breathe deeply, inhaling the beautiful aromas of Green. Place the Bottles on your Heart Chakra, or wherever they feel best on or around your body. To accelerate the healing and intensify the saturation of the Green frequencies, place a small flashlight at the base or behind the Bottle, causing the colour to illuminate. Auracle's Colours may be left on the body for any length of time desired, accompanied by any other colours of choice. It is not recommended or necessary to saturate your energy field with the colours for more than 20-30 minutes at a time **if using flashlights**. Conscious shifts may occur immediately depending on the level of healing called in by the soul. All experiences are unique.

Reflections of Balance Through Meditation: While sitting or lying down, place the Bottle/Bottles on or around your body as directed above. Close your eyes and feel the Green frequency saturating your Heart, and your entire being. As this beautiful light is flowing through your energy field, visualize the Auracle's Symbol radiating from your Heart Chakra out into the Universe bringing in the energies of expansion and growth. This will create a feeling of "lightness" and love, and a flow of "magickal" energies of an opened Heart throughout your body. Continuing to do meditations with the Green Bottles will bring much needed changes into your life, and the freshness of a new beginning.

Keynote: To hold a baby, to hug a tree, to play with a sweet fuzzy puppy or a soft little kitten will help to awaken the "unconditional" Heart. It is the willingness for an open Heart that allows the healing to occur. As the Heart is the bridge between the upper and lower Chakras, so it is the center of truth, our truth and our guidance from God, our Guides and the Universe.

In the Heart is where the "I" becomes "we" as we move up from the independence of the Solar Plexus and become conscious of sharing life with other beings in the world. It is here that we begin to express our desire to love and be loved by others..."Our Cup Runneth Over" with love, to fill our Hearts.

Royal Turquoise Bottle

Other Names: Ananda-Khanda center, The "Love" center, or The "Higher Heart".

Location: Lies closer to the Heart on the right side between the Heart and Throat Chakras.

Colour: Turquoise

Element: Air/Ether

Opposite Colour: Coral

Gems/Minerals: Turquoise, Apophyllite Pyramid, Aquamarine

Symbolism: The wisdom and technology of Atlantis, crystals, the sea, dolphins (group mind) and the water bearer representing the Age of Aquarians.

Archetypes: Artist/poet, Hermit, Scientist (Functional), Misanthropist, Mad Scientist (Dysfunctional)

Area of Consciousness: Astral/Etheric bodies

Governs: Our connection to creativity, the stars, dolphins and our inner guidance/inner teacher.

Physical Attributes: Heart, throat, lungs, thymus, upper neck, shoulders (especially on the right side), related to circulation and regeneration and revitalization around the entire Heart area.

Harmonious Energy: Optimism, childlike in the positive sense (playful like a dolphin), has strong intuition having to do with feeling and trusts it, has a gift for higher technologies (possible memories of Atlantis), foreign languages, communication through mass media, speaks from matters of the Heart, uses positive emotional expression, deeply connected to Angels and Divas, loves mythology, expresses creativity beyond verbal (dance, music, writing, painting), has an affinity to stars (concerning astronomy and astrology), has a gift for teaching and speaking to large audiences, has a connection to ET's, a multidimensional being.

Dysfunctional Energy: Feelings of isolation like a hermit (in the negative sense), fears communication of all kinds, may have experienced a broken Heart which never fully healed (especially in a love relationship), inability to express feelings, has "writer's block", inability to create, dislikes crowds, feels left out/not good enough to join others, stage fright, dislikes higher technologies, overwhelmed by sadness, grief and or guilt, fears ET's.

Illness: Bronchitis, asthma and all problems in the chest area, problems with the thymus, cardiac rhythm, speech impediments, fever, swelling and circulatory disorders.

Using Your Royal and Illumination Turquoise Bottles: When using Auracle's Colours, always face the Symbol on the Bottle towards your body. Shake the Bottle thoroughly, and spray the energies around the body from head to toe. Breathe deeply, inhaling the beautiful aromas of Turquoise. Place the Bottles on the right side of the Heart Chakra, under the right clavicle (the Higher Heart), or wherever they feel best on or around your body. To accelerate the healing and intensify the Turquoise frequencies, place a small flashlight at the base or behind the Bottle causing the colour to illuminate. Auracle's Colours may be left on the body for any length of time desired, accompanied by any other colours of choice. It is not recommended or necessary to saturate your energy field with the colours for more than 20-30 minutes at a time **if using flashlights**. Conscious shifts may occur immediately depending on the level of healing called in by the soul. All experiences are unique.

Reflections of Balance Through Meditation: While sitting or lying down, place the Bottle/Bottles on or around your body as directed above. Close your eyes and visualize yourself lying in the center of a translucent cave made of Turquoise crystals, seeing and feeling the Sun's rays penetrating into your body. Let this energy of expression, and creation, saturate your energy field. During this process, you may feel pain being removed from your Heart and or Lungs, as this is the "Higher Heart" where most grief and guilt are suppressed.

By allowing the Turquoise to saturate your energy field, it will help to boost the immune system, and over a period of time, it will become easier to express repressed feelings, and literally help you to "get things off your chest", making your "heavy Heart" lighter.

Keynote: "The truth shall set you free" are the ancient words that have echoed in our Hearts from many Moons ago. Why must we speak the truth, and to whom do we speak it? The answers we seek can be found within our Hearts, which is where what is true and what is truth lie within our being. Inner guidance comes to us through the Heart. If we don't listen and betray what we know in our soul to be true we will suffer. Self-betrayal can show itself in the emotion of guilt. Guilt is self-anger directly related to our choices. If we allow ourselves to be put in or stay in a situation that no longer serves us, we become very angry with ourselves because what we are continuing to do is wrong. Guilt is an emotion so powerful that if not dealt with can destroy our entire immune system in a "Heartbeat", literally.

Remember, the Ananda-Khanda center or "Higher Heart" is about the innermost expression of feeling and creation. It is about being honest, truthful and getting "clear" with ourselves and others in all areas in our lives no matter what the outcome. This can help to eliminate any unnecessary suffering physically, emotionally, mentally and spiritually.

When working with the Turquoise Bottle, ask yourself this question; how much is it worth getting ill for another human being because we are too afraid to stand up for ourselves and speak the truth? "Keeping quiet" and "not rocking the boat" is no longer acceptable and clearly not the answer. Being true to yourself is. For those who don't like it, it is just another indicator that they do not belong in your life anymore. Listen to your Heart.

By calling upon the Turquoise, we invoke the Archangelic realm of protection to hold us safe whilst going through the necessary changes we have asked of the Universe. Inner guidance is the ability to truly hear your Angels and Guides directing you into higher places, always pushing you to extend your boundaries of greatness…and yes, this will mean change. People are afraid of change, but it is the stagnation that makes you suffer and live your life in pain. Don't be blind. Open your Hearts and listen with every cell of your being to the messages you are being given and then have the courage to follow through with them.

The more we dive into our emotions and express them creatively and truthfully, the more we are able to see, feel and know the beauty of who we are.

Royal Blue Bottle

Other Names: Throat Chakra, Visuddha (Sanskrit)

Location: Base of the Throat Chakra

Colour: Blue

Verb: I speak

Sense: Sound

Element: Ether/Sound

Opposite Colour: Orange

Gems/Minerals: Lapis Lazuli, Sapphire, Blue Diamond, Angelite, Blue Lace Agate, Blue Tanzanite, Light Blue Tourmaline, Herkimer Diamond

Symbolism: Mother Mary (loving peace and protection), the clear Blue skies…"out of the Blue" (connection to the Divine), Water (baptism, blessing, spiritual cleansing)

Archetypes: Leader/Mentor/Goddess (Functional), Follower/Puppet (Dysfunctional)

Area of Consciousness: Etheric Body

Governs: Expression of ideas and feelings through communication. If expressed artistically it would be through music, art, poetry, writing and dance.

Physical Attributes: Thyroid, parathyroid, throat, neck, lungs, vocal cords, bronchial apparatus (everything having to do with communication).

Harmonious Energy: Faith, ability to go "internal" and meditate to experience Divine energy/bliss, ability to communicate thoughts, ideas, feelings, serene, peaceful, uses authority well, patience, protectiveness, calmness, nurturing, self-knowledge, willpower, discipline, leadership, diplomacy, intuition.

Dysfunctional Energy: Silence, introversion, irresponsible, addictive, unable to surrender (let go, let God…yielding our Will to Divine Will), deficient of nurturing energy, paranoid, arrogant, self-righteous, depressed, timid, manipulative, unable to express thoughts, ideas, feelings, can talk too much, frigidity, weak.

Illness: Communication/speech problems, chronic sore throat, thyroid and immune system disorders, scoliosis, laryngitis, swollen glands, mouth ulcers.

Using Your Royal and Illumination Blue Bottles: When using Auracle's Colours, always face the Symbol on the Bottles towards your body. Shake the Bottles thoroughly, and spray the energies around the body from head to toe. Breathe deeply, inhaling the beautiful aromas of Blue. Place the Bottles at the base of the Throat, sitting just below the clavicles, or wherever they feel best on or around your body. You may also place Bottles on the left and right side of your neck. To accelerate the healing and intensify the saturation of the Blue frequencies, place a small flashlight at the base or behind each Bottle, causing the colour to illuminate. Auracle's Colours may be left on the body for any length of time desired, accompanied by any other colours of choice. It is not recommended or necessary to saturate your energy field with the colours for more than 20-30 minutes at a time **if using flashlights**. Conscious shifts may occur immediately depending on the level of healing called in by the soul. All experiences are unique.

Reflections of Balance Through Meditation: While sitting or lying down, place the Bottle/Bottles on or around the body as directed above. Close your eyes and see yourself floating gracefully on a raft under a crystal Blue sky in the middle of the Blue, glistening, Mediterranean Sea. Feel the peacefulness through the flow of the ocean gently rocking you back and forth as you "let go", allowing your arms and legs to flow freely. As you are doing this, be aware of the Blue frequencies penetrating your Throat/ neck area. At first, it is common to feel a "lump" in your Throat, or to feel energy "pulling" in certain areas of the neck.

If so, continue to relax, float, and feel the Blue frequency of peace flowing around your Throat and through your body. As the Blue light continues to saturate your energy field, be aware of the sensation of feeling nurtured and safe, floating in the womb of the ocean.

It might be helpful to repeat this meditation daily until the energy in your Throat opens up completely. The more closely connected to the Divine you become through using the Blue frequency, the more you will feel true "FAITH" and eliminate fear in your Heart.

Keynote: Another suggestion to help bring in the Blue frequencies to heal the Throat would be to sing, to chant and most definitely to laugh. Some of the greatest singers, spiritual leaders and comedians of present are extremely introverted, yet they have chosen these paths to express the many ways the voice can be heard to help heal themselves physically, mentally, emotionally and spiritually.

Singing and chanting are the "music of the spheres" heard by our Guides and Angels and laughter is the light from which they come. The Throat Chakra is the place where we align ourselves with Universal energy, surrendering our Will to Divine Will. It is the place where we take responsibility for who we are and not blaming it on others for the choices we make, or the consequences we have suffered as per those choices. The more we raise our own vibration to connect into these energies through the Blue frequency, the more it enables us to "hear" our guidance from the Divine, i.e., messages from "out of the Blue". It is this connection that helps us to heal and stay on our life path.

Remember, **faith** is the opposite of **fear**, which means, "Let Go, Let God" and trust the process. Don't attempt to interject your control into Divine process, as your "Will"

will never win, but only create chaos and struggle. Allow your Guides to "lead" you instead of "push" you. They know more than you, so have faith and listen to what they are saying…even, and especially if it requires you to change your life.

Are you ready to listen? Then let go, and feel the peacefulness enter your Heart.

Royal Indigo Bottle

Other Names: Third Eye, Brow, Ajna (Sanskrit)

Location: Between the eyebrows (behind the forehead)

Colour: Indigo (deep Blue/Violet)

Verb: I see

Sense: This level is referred to the sixth sense describing psychic or intuitive abilities

Element: Light, Electrical/Telepathic energy

Opposite Colour: Gold

Gems/Minerals: Azurite, Lapis Lazuli, Deep Blue Tourmaline

Symbolism: Isis (Universal Mother/Goddess/Creator/Protector), King David (Leader of the Jews), the Unicorn (The magick of the awakened third eye)

Archetypes: High Priestess, Magician, Mystic, Shaman, Crone (Functional), Intellect (Dysfunctional)

Area of Consciousness: Celestial Body

Governs: Spirituality, self-realization, higher intuition, visualization, Power of the mind: What is illusion and what is truth.

Physical Attributes: Pituitary gland, eyes, ears, nose.

Harmonious Energy: Deep wisdom, inner vision, inner illumination, psychic awareness/powers (clairvoyance, clairsentience, clairaudience), can receive guidance through dreams and symbols, dignity, integrity, tranquility, charisma, detachment from unnecessary energies in the spiritual or physical worlds, projection of will, imagination, intellect, transformation at the deepest levels of the conscious and subconscious, inspiration, trustworthiness, the ability to recognize the "magick" in ones' life moment by moment.

Dysfunctional Energy: Extreme isolation, manipulation, the "shadow" side or "dark night of the soul" (what we hide from the world), arrogance, opinionated, proud, authoritarian, egomaniac, afraid of success, extreme depression, illusion, judgmental, over-intellectualize, mental over-stimulation.

Illness: Psychic exhaustion, mental illness, hormonal imbalance, brain tumor, neurological disturbances, blindness, deafness, learning disabilities, confusion, paranoia, resistance to things as they are or need to be, facing unresolved fears.

<u>Using Your Royal and Illumination Indigo Bottles</u>: When using Auracle's Colours, always face the Symbol on the Bottle towards your body. Shake the Bottle thoroughly, and spray the energies around the body from head to toe. Breathe deeply, inhaling the beautiful aromas of Indigo. Place either of the Bottles on the Third Eye between the brows, or wherever they feel best on or around your body. If using both Royal and Illumination Bottles, place them on the left and right side of your temples. To accelerate the healing and intensify the saturation of the Indigo frequencies, place a small flashlight at the base or behind each Bottle, causing the colours to illuminate. You may also hold the Indigo Bottles over your Third Eye and look into **INDIRECT** Sunlight. Auracle's Colours may be left on the body for any length of time desired, accompanied by any other colours of choice. It is not recommended or necessary to saturate your energy field with the colours for more than 20-30 minutes at a time **if using flashlights**. Conscious shifts may occur immediately depending on the level of healing called in by the soul. All experiences are unique.

<u>Reflections of Balance Through Meditation</u>: While sitting or lying down, place the Bottles on or around your body as directed above. Close your eyes, relax and feel the Indigo energies penetrating deeply into your Third Eye. Visualize a beautiful Indigo star, radiating from your Third Eye with rays that extend out like the Sun...or an Indigo flame that burns eternally, always in motion. You may initially feel heaviness or pulsations of energy movement between your brows, which is normal. You may experience the feeling of "isolation", or a sensation of floating in the abyss during this meditation. Should fear arise, continue to breathe slowly allowing the tranquil frequencies of Indigo to saturate your energy field. Know you are completely protected by your Guides, and the Universe itself.

Be prepared to experience very deep and detailed dreams while using either Indigo Bottles. These Bottles will assist you in unveiling the Symbols in your dreams, helping you to clearly see your life's purpose, continuing on to the next level.

<u>Keynote</u>: The Indigo ray is our connection into the abyss as vast and mystical as the Universe itself. It is our connection into the God/Goddess energies within. It is also the darkness of which we fear. Through meditation we bring in the possibility of feeling "safe" enough to see clearly what lies ahead and to hear our orders issued from above. It is our journey into the darkness to manifest the light, for only when we do this can we fulfill our Blueprint. It is a journey we must take alone.

Royal Violet Bottle

Other Names: Crown Chakra, the "I Am" Center, Sahasrara (Sanskrit)

Location: At the top of the head

Colour: Pale Violet, White/Violet, Violet/Gold

Verb: I know

Sense: None

Element: Thought, Cosmic Energy

Opposite Colour: Yellow

Gems/Minerals: Amethyst, Violet Tourmaline, Actinolite, Purperite, Violet Tanzanite, Black Tourmaline, Herkimer Diamond

Symbolism: The Violet Flame of Transmutation

Archetypes: Wizard, Healer, Visionary (Functional), Victim, Egotist, Charlatan (Dysfunctional)

Area of Consciousness: Ketheric Body (where we merge with God and "All That Is")

Governs: The search for our spirituality, to seek and connect the Divine in all we do.

Physical Attributes: Skull, pineal gland, production of mucus

Harmonious Energy: Visionary leader, the Healer/ Miracle worker, the need to serve human kind through Divine loving energy, the ability to access gateways into other worlds and to understand that there is a presence higher than ourselves guiding us, being conscious of our unity with the Divine, having self dignity, self honor, self respect, illumination, reflective, possess strong psychic abilities, and can bring into balance the male and female energy within the self.

Dysfunctional Energy: Poverty mentality/has difficulty manifesting in the material world, victim (always blaming others for their problems and never changing because of it), Martyr, contemplates too much, too much "in the head", over intellectual, arrogant, suicidal, suffers too much, feels grief, feels alone and withdrawn, incapable of making decisions.

Illness: Stress, migraine headaches, psychosis, manic depression, bone cancer, paralysis, genetic disorders, multiple sclerosis, hysteria, insanity.

Using Your Royal and Illumination Violet Bottles: When using Auracle's Colours, always face the Symbol on the Bottle towards your body. Shake the Bottle thoroughly and spray the energies around the body from head to toe. Breathe deeply, inhaling the beautiful aromas of Violet. Place the Bottles around or at the top of your Crown, or wherever they feel best on or around your body. To accelerate the healing and intensify the saturation of the Violet frequencies, place a small flashlight at the base or behind each Bottle, causing the colour to illuminate. Auracle's Colours may be left on the body for any length of time desired, accompanied by any other colours of choice. It is not recommended or necessary to saturate your energy field with the colours for more than 20-30 minutes at a time **if using flashlights**. Conscious shifts may occur immediately depending on the level of healing called in by the soul. All experiences are unique.

Reflections of Balance Through Meditation: While sitting or lying down, place the Bottle/Bottles on or around your body as directed above. Close your eyes and visualize lying in an eternal field of Violets, surrounded by an illuminated Violet mist, gently moving through the breeze above you. Dewdrops sit on each pedal of every flower, glistening in the Sun like amethyst crystals. Slowly, out of the mist appears a tall thin man with long White hair and a beard walking towards you. He is wearing a beautiful Violet robe and carries in his right hand a magickal staff. There is a brilliant crystal of White/Violet light glowing at the top. His eyes sparkle, and his face speaks of wisdom, peace, and love. He reveals these energies as the Violet mist gently blows his hood back and forth as he approaches your energy field. He is no ordinary man, who stands before you now…He is Merlin. Merlin has come to help you awaken your Crown energies by stimulating the Violet light within your soul.

Merlin reaches over your body and touches the tip of your Crown with the crystal atop his staff. As he touches you, you feel an explosion of White/Violet light bursting out of your Crown into the Universe. Feel the illuminated Violet rays extend from your Crown to the Divine and reflect back to you as if you have become one with the light. This is a beautiful way to merge with the Universe and align yourself with the God/Goddess energies.

Keynote: The journey of the soul is to ultimately realize that there is no separation between us, and the energies of God/Goddess and All That Is. It is through meditation that we create the possibilities of experiencing illumination through Divine love. Meditation can help us to transcend our thoughts, illusions, cravings, aversions, and our emotions. It can also help us change our cellular patterns from having feelings of aloneness to those of ALL-ONE-NESS. In this state of being we can recognize and ultimately realize our reason for living.

Illumination Red (Pink) Bottle

Other Names: Heart Chakra

Location: Pink moves through all Chakras as it is unconditional and exists in every cell of our being

Colour: Light Pink

Element: Earth/Cosmic Energy

Opposite Colour: Illumination Green

Gems/Minerals: Pink Diamond, Opal, Rose Pink Tourmaline, Rose Quartz, Danburite Pink

Symbolism: A Pink rose, a newborn sentient being representing innocence and beauty... a child, a puppy, a kitten, a lamb.

Archetypes: The Mother, the Fool, the Child

Area of Consciousness: All levels

Governs: Our ability to embrace ourselves, and others unconditionally with kindness and love.

Physical Attributes: Pink works through the entire body affecting every function from the hormones and reproductive system in the Root Chakra to eyesight and hearing in the Crown Chakra.

Harmonious Energy: Romantic, loving, warm, shows kindness, gentleness, good listener, has a positive attitude, extremely feminine, exudes "Mother Love", unconditional in nature, compassionate, sensitive, creative (especially through music), imaginative, able to give and receive tenderness, forgiving, has a strong sense of companionship, honor and harmony, is faithful and believes in fidelity, sexually charged love (may practice Tantra), has a deep love for art and beauty, affectionate, intuitive.

Dysfunctional Energy: Smother-love, vulnerable, manipulative, immature, dishonest, believes they are undeserving of love and have no love to give (probably due to a loveless childhood and don't know how), feels no joy, negative attitude, helpless, "too" giving, sexually promiscuous, are open to being wounded by others, can be overly feminine or in denial of the feminine aspect altogether, selfish, unable to receive love and kindness from self or others.

Illness: Hormonal and reproductive problems, deafness

Using Your Illumination Pink Bottle: When using Auracle's Colours, always face the Symbol on the Bottle towards your body. Shake the Bottle thoroughly, and spray the energies around the body from head to toe. Breathe deeply, inhaling the beautiful aromas of Pink. Since Pink is "unconditional", it can be placed anywhere on the body, whether it be on the Root, Solar Plexus or Heart Chakras, etc. There is no particular Chakra it belongs to. Therefore, place the Bottle wherever it feels best on your body. To accelerate the healing and intensify the Pink frequencies, place a small flashlight at the base or behind the Bottle, causing the colour to illuminate. Auracle's Colours may be left on the body for any length of time desired, accompanied by any other colours of choice. It is not recommended or necessary to saturate your energy field with the colours for more than 20-30 minutes at a time **if using flashlights**. Conscious shifts may occur immediately depending on the level of healing called in by the soul. All experiences are unique.

Reflections of Balance Through Meditation: While sitting or lying down, place the Bottle/Bottles on or around your body as directed above. Since Pink is unconditional it can be placed anywhere on the body. Recommendations would be the Heart (needing unconditional love) and Root Chakras (feminine/hormonal issues).

Close your eyes and allow the Pink light of unconditional love move through your body. Let this feeling saturate every cell of your being, expanding through each of your Chakras from Root to Crown. As you feel the light moving through cells, visualize your entire body glowing Pink, with Pink rays of light shooting from your body out into the Universe. To bring another level of unconditional love into your body, imagine holding a newborn baby, a puppy or a kitten on your Heart while doing this meditation. Feel their love coming back to you, and radiate this love back to them. It will bring in another dimension of love to help your Heart to awaken and heal. You might begin to feel lighter and you might even begin to cry, for this is a reminder of how we came into this world…innocent, with no expectations, and filled with love. You may also hold the Pink Bottle over your Heart and call upon your Angels to assist you in bringing unconditional love, compassion and forgiveness into your soul. You will feel it right away through the expansion and calmness of your Heart.

Keynote: Love is the antidote to fear and can help us to fill the holes that have made us feel empty in our Hearts, in our lives, in our very souls. It is the unconditional love that can help to remind us of who we are…Who We Truly Are…and not a melting pot of everyone else's perceptions. Love can help us to recover what has long since been lost, possibly from our childhood, and still yet…from many Moons ago. Listen to your Guides and trust the Universe, for they are showing you the way back to your soul. Live and be present in every moment so that you may "hear" their beautiful and mystical music playing in your ears. Be open to love… and to seeing yourself with new eyes.

An Extra Loving Note: This is the Bottle to use to help gently guide you through a grieving process. Pink, being unconditional, nurtures the Heart and helps the pain of losing a loved one, or animal, by filling your Heart back up with light.

A Soothing Meditation For Loss: Holding the Pink Bottle to your Heart, close your eyes and use your senses to see, smell, hear and connect with the presence of your loved ones who have crossed over. As the Pink light saturates your body, feel the comfort of their spirits around you. You have only to pick up the Bottle, hold it to your Heart, and call them in to be with you anytime you desire. They will hear your Heart and answer through their presence.

Illumination Clear Bottle

Other Names: None

Location: Clear or "White" moves through all Chakras as it is the reflection of all colours.

Element: Ethereal/Cosmic Energy

Gems/Minerals: Opal, Quartz Crystal, Herkimer Diamond

Symbolism: The Moon, the Holy Ghost, the White Rose (a sign of integrity, honesty, simplicity and truth), the Mirror (for deep reflection in which we can recognize ourselves), the Silver Sword (cutting away what we do not need).

Archetypes: The Virgin, Excalibur, Lady of the Lake

Area of Consciousness: All levels

Governs: Our ability to see that we are Pure Light…to find the light within ourselves.

Physical Attributes: Clear or White works through all Chakras of the body, for it's purpose is detoxification on all levels (physically, emotionally, mentally, spiritually).

Harmonious Energy: Innocence, spirituality, ordination, baptism, clarity, spiritual protection, healing abilities, is aware of a higher power, could be a spiritual teacher, has determination, brilliance, expansion, purity, wholeness.

Dysfunctional Energy: Suffers endlessly, carries the weight of too many, unshed tears, needing to be "too" perfect, karmic absolution, emptiness, sitting in one's shadow.

Illness: Toxicity on all levels (physically, emotionally, mentally, spiritually).

Using Your Illumination Clear Bottle: When using Auracle's Colours, always face the Symbol on the Bottle towards your body. Shake the Bottle thoroughly, and spray the energies around the body from head to toe. Breathe deeply, inhaling the beautiful aromas of Clear/White. Since Clear or White are the reflections of all colours, this Bottle can be placed anywhere on or around your body. Listen to your intuition, as you may want to hold the Bottle on your Heart Chakra, or place it wherever you feel the light is needed for detoxification as well as helping you through the process of releasing pain and tears.

To accelerate the healing and intensify the saturation of the Clear or White frequency, place a small flashlight at the base or behind the Bottle, causing the Bottle to illuminate. Auracle's Colours may be left on the body for any length of time desired, accompanied by any other colours of choice. It is not recommended or necessary to saturate your energy field with the colours for more than 20-30 minutes at a time **if using flashlights**. Conscious shifts may occur immediately depending on the level of healing called in by the soul. All experiences are unique.

Reflections of Balance Through Meditation: While sitting or lying down, place the Bottle/Bottles on or around your body as directed above. Close your eyes and call upon your Angels, Archangels, Masters, Faeries and other Light Beings, whomever you feel present, or would like to connect with spiritually.

Visualize their energies about three feet above your left and right shoulders as well as above your Crown Chakra. Each of them is holding a sacred Silver chalice filled with liquid, crystalline light, and begins to pour this magickal light over your body as if you were standing under a beautiful and glistening white waterfall, ever flowing and endless.

Imagine these waters filled with luminous light penetrating your tissues, organs, muscles, cells and bones. Allow the toxic energies, tears and pain to flow down from your body and be washed into the earth. Feel the coolness of the Divine light penetrating deeper into your body.

Visualize the crystal water flowing down from your Crown Chakra into the rest of the body, and as the light passes through each Chakra, it becomes luminous, shining like a diamond with rays of light exploding outward like rays from the Sun. It will appear to you as if you were standing in front of a bright Sunlit window, yet even with your eyes closed, the light still penetrates. You may experience that some Chakras will be easier to fill with light than others.

If possible, stay on the Chakras you are experiencing difficulties with. It may take several meditations to get to a point where you give yourself permission to shine the light on that, which has remained in the dark possibly from this lifetime or others. You may even begin to cry as the Chakras are dispelling old memories of suffering, as Clear also represents unshed tears.

Filling your body with light and becoming "clear" will allow newer and brighter energies to descend through your Crown. As you continue with this meditation, or various others using the Clear Bottle, you will notice an influx of creative ideas and new thoughts coming through.

Keynote: Working with the Clear energy allows us to recognize our many different levels of consciousness, as Clear is the ray which contains and is a reflection of all colours. By embracing our many complexities and utilizing Divine energies given to us by the Universe, it then becomes possible that we can sculpt a diamond out of ourselves, becoming luminous, and ever brilliant.

Harmonization of Colour

Royal and Illumination Bottles

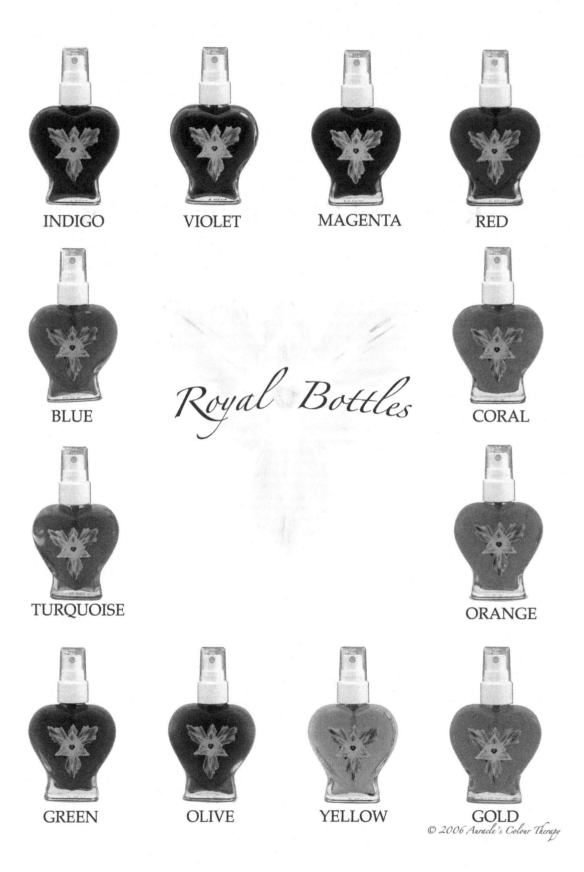

INDIGO   VIOLET   MAGENTA   RED

BLUE   *Royal Bottles*   CORAL

TURQUOISE   ORANGE

GREEN   OLIVE   YELLOW   GOLD

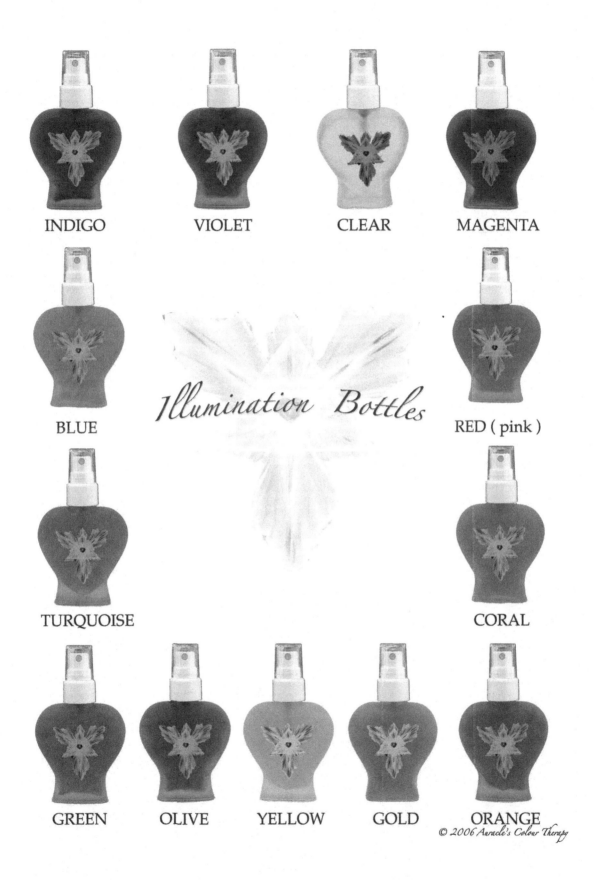

INDIGO   VIOLET   CLEAR   MAGENTA

BLUE   *Illumination Bottles*   RED (pink)

TURQUOISE   CORAL

GREEN   OLIVE   YELLOW   GOLD   ORANGE

© 2006 Auracle's Colour Therapy

The Magickal History of Colour

Chapter I

What is Colour Therapy?

Colour or "Chromotherapy" is the theraputic use of light and colour to heal imbalance or disease. Every substance on earth contains a colour. All humans contain the full spectrum of colours within their bodies, otherwise known as the "rainbow".

Light is derived from the Sun and is the reflection of all colours, whereas black has no reflection, as it is the absorption of all colours. The Sunlight has the full spectrum of rainbow colours (Red, Orange, Yellow, Green, Blue, Indigo, and Violet), each of which align with our entire physical, emotional, mental and spiritual being. It would make sense then, if our entire cellular structure, organs, tissues, bones, etc. are made up of the complete spectrum of colours, to stay healthy and prevent dis-ease would require all colours within our bodies be at their highest level of vibrancy. This can be achieved through receiving Sunlight itself, which of course, contains all colours of the rainbow. To understand this better, we will show how colour works.

Colour, in essence, is light split into different wavelengths which vibrate at different speeds and frequencies, octaves or tones. Long waves include radio and infrared, and are the warmer colours such as Red, Orange and Yellow, which add energy or stimulate. These colours carry more of an intensity. Short waves include ultraviolet, gamma and x-ray, which are cooler, subtler in nature and can decrease life energy or sedate. Red has a longer wavelength and travels slower. Violet has a shorter wave, therefore travels faster. An example would be that most of us have experienced from time to time, x-rays throughout our lives. Notice that when the x-rays are taken that they are finished within seconds. This is because the "violet ray" has a short wavelength, thus it moves more quickly. *See in diagram A.*

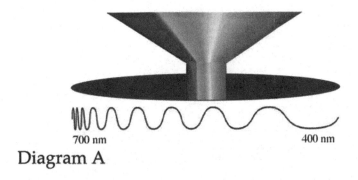

700 nm   400 nm

Diagram A

Sir Isaac Newton discovered the spectrum in 1666 as he passed light through a prism. He found because of the different wavelengths it would cause the light to bend in different directions, thus causing the colours to separate out. This is something, however, that the Egyptians discovered several thousands of years before. *See in diagram B.*

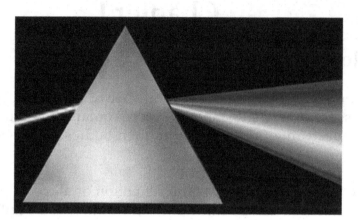

Diagram B

Each colour seen above has its own purpose and effect on every human being and living organism. This will be discussed further in detail throughout the book.

Chapter II

Ancient Wisdom Brought Forth to Healing Techniques in the Present

The East Indian Ayuvedic ("Ayur" means "life" and "veda" means "science") system of Tridosha or the Three Doshas (Pitta, Vata, and Kapha) encorporate the Chakras (see explanation below) for balancing the entire being. The doshas determine the capacity of a person's health, but also are determined by the forces of the world around them. For instance, we are all different. The doshas determine what type you are by the following: Do you like spicy or mild food, do you like hot or cold weather, are you quick or slow moving, do you get hot easily or are you always cold, do you lose your temper quickly or are you normally very calm, are you small, medium or large boned…etc. I think you get the idea.

In Traditional Chinese Medicine, which dates back over five thousand years, each organ of the body is also associated with a specific colour and has negative and positive sounds. As mentioned previously, the body is divided into twelve regions or meridians relating to each organ. Each is associated with its own specific colour. These regions are observed for coloration or discoloration to diagnose ill-health. Asian medicine teaches us that our bodies have meridians (circuits of energy that form lines similar to a road map), which carry energy throughout our system connecting with every major organ. When blockages occur in these meridians, disease will follow. It has been their belief for over 2,000 years that perfect health and spiritual enlightenment can be attained through the mastering the art of circulating "Gold light" throughout the body, Gold being connected to inner wisdom, strength, will power, abundance, honour, confidence, enlightenment and self- mastery. Gold is also the colour that throughout history can be seen painted over the Saints, Masters and Angels as halos depicting their connections to the Divine.

Chapter III

The History of Colour

"Colour transmits itself to us as visual vibration." *John Anthony West, Egyptologist.*

Colour healing was used in Ancient Egypt, Babylonia, Greece, Rome, China and India amongst other major cultures.

However, it was the Ancient Egyptian Mythology where chromotherapy was brought into consciousness by the God Djehuti (pronounced Tehuti). Djehuti was known to the Greeks as Thoth or Hermes Trimegistus (trimegistus means thrice greatest). Djehuti or Thoth/Hermes to both Egyptians and Greeks was the Lord of Wisdom (hidden knowledge) and Learning, a scribe to the Gods, the inventor of Hieroglyphics, and the one who brought them mysticism and magick. It was Hermes who brought forth his teachings onto the famous *"Emerald Tablets"* from a single Emerald Tablet known as the *Corpus Hermetica*. These tablets contained formulas using colour, light, sound and other sacred teachings to help the acceleration of humanity. This is known as "Hermeticism", the science of the invisible, the hidden, the mysteries of what go beneath and beyond what the human eye can see or the human body can touch. It is the scientific knowledge and control of the invisible forces governing our souls in the material world.

Both Thoth and Hermes are associated with sacred writings, which revealed to humankind magick, writing, philosophy, science, astrology and the healing arts. It is said they brought the wisdom of light into the ancient mysteries of Egypt.

In the Hermetic (Egyptian/Greek) Traditions, it was common especially for the priests to use coloured healing stones, ointments, minerals, solarized (Sun infused) water, salves, dyes and clothing to help the soul achieve balance and treat disease. For this reason, colour was vital in the healing arts.

In the Ancient Egyptian city of Heliopolis, Greek for "City of the Sun", there were many healing temples known as "solariums", which made use of Sunlight separating into different spectral components or colours. It is said each room within the temples was lined with different coloured paints, crystals and gems. To add to the intensity of the experience, the temples were built with stones representing the different elements such as grantite (fire), sandstone (earth), limestone (water) and alabaster (air), placed in particular areas of each temple. This would accelerate ritualistic practices and healing processes as well as shift the consciousness of the soul.

When the Sun passed over the temples, the colours of the gems would illuminate, thereby, accelerating the healing process of the patient in the chamber through saturation of that particular colour. Each colour was used to treat a specific medical problem.

To the ancients who loved and worshipped the Sun, the colours within the rays of the Sunlight had very specific functions. Each colour was considered to show a different aspect of the Divine and influence different qualities of life. They knew that light was the primary source of longevity, and colour could restore peace of mind, balance the emotions, and release pain form the physical body.

Note: The *Emerald Tablets* are not actual Ancient Egyptian texts. They are thought to have originated in Atlantis, brought into Egypt by Thoth. However, the writings themselves are based upon and are consistent with the teachings within Ancient Egyptian texts. Although there are little or no remains of these solarium temples to be found, there was a recent uncovering in Cairo prior to the turn of the New Year of 2007.

Chapter IV

The Aesclepion Temples

The mythical roots of Asclepius (Asclepios or Aesculapius, known to the Romans) goes back before the 11th century B.C. He was born the son of the Greek god Apollo who was originally known as the "god of Medicine", until which time he passed his gifts via his mentor and teacher, Chiron, who taught him the art of healing using surgical methods, drugs, incantations and making magickal potions. Within a short period of time, Asclepius became a famous physician, a demi god, and a temple god in his own right.

There were approximately 420 shrines and temples of healing dedicated to Aesclepius known as Asclepia or Asclepions that were built throughout Ancient Greece, mostly found on the island of Kos, better known as the Island of Medicine, where people would come to find cures for their ailments (much like the modern journeys to Lourdes in France today). The most famous sanctuary was located in Epidaurus, situated in the northeastern Peloponnese, the seat of the early Mycenaean civilization.

In various temples were "colour halls", used much like the solarium temples in Egypt, generally being based upon the healing energies of the Sun, and colours coming from within the Suns light.

There were also "dream rooms" where seekers would go to sleep, go into their unconscious, or a state of "darkness" by the shadow of the Moon or alone by the darkness of the evening sky, and receive cures for their illness via the Gods. It is even said that occasionally Asclepius himself would appear with remedies needed for the soul to heal.

This process was known as "incubation" derived from the Latin word, in (on) cubare (to lie down), referring to the dream experience in the temple.

The order of priest physicians who controlled the sacred secrets of healing were called Asclepiadae. The teachings and worship of Asclepius spread throughout Rome around the 1st Century A.D., and continued until the sixth century.

Chapter V

Colour Therapy and Famous Historical Figures

Hippocrates (circa 470-400BC) known as the Father of Medicine, was a Greek physician born on the island of Kos, the Island of Medicine. He believed that colour was an outward expression of an internal pathological condition. He too, had discovered the different frequency levels of colours as he was known to use different coloured pastes to treat wounds.

Hippocrates wrote the famous *Doctrine of Humors*, which laid the foundation for modern medicine as we know it today. It was based on the four elements (air, water, fire, earth), each correlating to a different colour. By diagnosing the patient according to the colour variations of the hair, skin, eyes and bodily fluids, the illness or disease could be treated with more accuracy. Even today, especially in alternative medicine, this format of diagnosis is continued by observation of the colour of the skin, the eyes, the tongue and bodily fluids.

Pythagoras, a Greek philosopher (6th Century B.C.) developed theories of light and dark. 500 years before Christ, Pythagoras used colour extensively in his medical practices. He discovered, for instance, that the therapeutic effects of white violet would be completely different from that of a darker violet as they are each different frequencies or tones and respond to different physical, emotional, mental and spiritual aspects of the soul. It was through various modalities of healing energies including colour, sound (music), and poetry, that Pythagoras is said to have cured disease.

"The body of God is composed of the substance of light". *Pythagoras*

Aristotle (4th Century B.C.), a famous Greek philosopher, teacher to Alexander the Great and colleague of Hippocrates, developed theories of light and dark as did Pythagoras. He considered blue and yellow to be the only true primary colours, which related to polarities of all types: male and female, the Sun and the Moon, stimulus and sedation, expansion and contraction. As did Hippocrates, he associated colour with the four elements: fire, water, earth and air.

Aristotle had also experimented with various forms of coloured mixtures and concluded when coloured "light" was infused, the outcome would be the same as if it was mixed in paints…he was wrong. If yellow and blue "paints" are mixed together we will see green. However, if yellow and blue "lights" are infused we will see red.

(To experiment with this try shining a light through two bottles of yellow liquid and two bottles of blue liquid side by side like a stack of books, and pushed together…you'll see.)

Lets explore the relevance of these primary colours to us as humans. According to Vicky Wall, developer of Aura-Soma and mentioned further in this chapter, the significance of the Blue and the Yellow bringing in the Red (energetically), represent our three stars as we descend from spirit in the heavens into human form on Earth.

The Blue, signifying the heavens, represents our "*Soul Star*", existing above the Crown Chakra and is our connection to spirit/spiritual energy. The Yellow is our "*Incarnational Star*", located in the Solar Plexus (stomach region), and is our connections to our individuality or our true self, and mental energy. The Red is our "*Earth Star*", located below the feet and is our connection to life force or physical energy, and Earth itself. Thus, when the mind, body and soul stars are in alignment, we can realize our purpose for being in this world, living each moment with true peace and clarity.

We can see these three colours manifested in the Holy Trine: THE FATHER (the spiritual father and physical mother are Red), THE SON (the child is Yellow…the "Sun/fire", representing the light of wisdom and knowledge in the belly), and THE HOLY GHOST (spirit in pure form, from the heavens, i.e. "out of the Blue".)

If you were to light a match, you would see the same colours in the flame of Red, Yellow and Blue, as this also represents Universal Light, or the flame within man, since man is made in the image of God, and God is made of light.

The 1st Century AD, **Aurelius Cornelius Celsus** followed the doctrines established by *Hippocrates* and *Pythagoras*, which not only included using dyes, minerals, solarized waters, etc., but also included coloured plasters for healing purposes.

Avicenna, born Ibn Sina in Iran (980-1037) was an extraordinary philosopher, alchemist, mathematician, astronomer and physician. At the age of sixteen he had mastered the study of medicine, and by the age of twenty-one, being self-taught in most subjects, had become accomplished in all branches of formal education.

Avicennas first and most famous book was, *Al -Quanun fi al – Tibb* (The Canon of Medicine). It was the most consulted medical encyclopedia of its time, serving as chief guide for medical science in the west until the 17th century.

The Canon of Medicine contains substantial medical documentation regarding the use of colours and music (each note corresponding to a different Colour) as a guide to help with diagnosing illness as well as to cure it. For instance, Avicenna found red light and red herbs, which are the warmer element of the Sunlight to help anemia, paralysis and other dormant and chronic illnesses. He found this to correspond to the note "G". When conditions such as inflammation, nerves, sciatica, hemorrhaging of the lungs, Sunstroke, cerebrospinal meningitis and headaches were exposed to violet and blue light, the cooler element of the Sunlight, it had a soothing and sedate effect and corresponded to the note "C".

Avicenna took it further by studying the breath associating specific colours to each organ. He felt that breath or "vital force" is a link between the spirit, body and soul. He discovered that each emotion within the organs generate particular breathing patterns and emotional changes were directly correlated to altering blood states. His conclusion was to find the organ and heal the emotion causing the imbalance with the appropriate colour.

To have perfect health, one would have to maintain a perfect state of balance within the elements of the body and environment. If there is a change at the elemental level, there will be a change in the physical process. This corresponds to the *"Doctrine of Humors"* aforementioned written by Hippocrates, discussing the elements (air, fire, water and earth), their association to each organ, their colours and how this relates to proper diagnosis and healing of the body.

Avicenna knew that to restore health, the causes of both health and disease must be determined. He also recognized that man and nature are deeply connected, and the importance of understanding this union to maintain a perfect state of being, physically, emotionally, mentally and spiritually.

Paracelsus (1493-1541), a famous Swiss doctor, alchemist, a mystic and a healer placed particular importance on the role of colour in healing. He used plants and herbs with the appropriate colour to heal illness. Paracelsus incorporated "liquid Gold" into many of his treatments and medicines with effective results. As did Hippocrates, Paracelsus associated each organ with the elements and their meanings, of air (coolness), fire (heat), water (wetness) and earth (dryness) into proper diagnosis and treatment of his patients. Paracelsus was the contemporary of some very famous figures in the Renaissance such as Copernicus, Martin Luther and Leonardo da Vinci.

Sir Issac Newton (1642-1727) the first to pass light through a prism and formed the theory that light is made of all colours. Newton also composed a musical or "diatonic" scale in which each colour had a correlating note, such as Red (C), Orange (D), Yellow (E), Green (F), Blue (G), Indigo (A), Violet (B).

In 1672 Newton published his first controversial paper on colour theory, and in 1712 published his work in his Book 1 "Opticks", describing his invention of the first reflecting telescope. He was also one of the foremost modern day alchemists who, more than working with what is known as modern day science, studied Hermeticism.

"I have seen farther than other men…it is by standing on the shoulders of giants". *Sir Issac Newton*

Johann Wolfgang von Goethe (1749-1832) was a famous German poet, scientist and novelist. Goethe intended to bring in a unity of physical knowledge combined with all aspects of natural science. His book entitled "Theory of Colours" documents his work amounting to 2000 pages. *Theory of Colours* was an advanced study of light and dark, which surpassed Newton's theories 100 years later. He discovered that within the seemingly colourless light, all colours exist already. So, when passing light through a prism it simply causes the colours to reveal themselves. Further, Goethe discovered that if one were to look directly through the light, that the colours would actually appear on the borders or the edges of where the light and dark flow together. In other words, all colours exist between light and dark, as do they exist within the human soul, as the soul is made of light.

Rudolph Steiner (1861-1925) was a philosopher, a mystic, a visionary, a novelist and a scientific researcher of spiritual dimensions in which colour played an important role. Rudolph described the importance of colour in the following quote:

"Colour Therapy or Chromotherapy has been successfully used since ancient times and has been a part of medical practice for many centuries past. Colour is the soul of nature and by experiencing the life of colour, we participate in this soul".

He brought his philosophy of what he called "anthroposophy" or the "spiritual science" into the world. He wrote many books and gave over 6,000 lectures on such subjects as religion, occultism, farming (based on a holistic approach to nutrition), child education, life between death and re-birth, and how to develop spiritual sight in which he included various forms of meditations.

Rudolph was able to see into other dimensions, and through the "light" he was able to see all colours of the rainbow emanating from all beings. He was also able to hear the tones that spoke to him through each colour, as each colour has its own frequency.

The famous Steiner Waldorf Schools were developed and based on his philosophies as a spiritual scientist. In every school, the classrooms are painted and textured according to the various moods and developmental stages of the children. This has a tremendous impact on the child's physical, emotional, mental and spiritual well- being. There are approximately 600 schools located in over 32 countries with nearly 150,000 students in attendance continuing to grow around the world today.

Rudolph saw the necessary connection between love (Pink) and wisdom (Gold), together equaling intelligence of the Heart, to push the human personality beyond its judgments and desires, which limit spiritual growth.

He knew what many masters have known for thousands of years, and what is still taught today by many spiritual visionaries and teachers…drop the "physical" needs, identity and illusions altogether. In other words, stop seeking from outside yourself that which you need to look within to obtain spiritual growth. When this is achieved and one looks within to find the light, then one will begin to see all humans as light beings with the colours of the rainbow radiating from every aura, thereby witnessing the sacred dance between the colours and the soul itself.

Edwin D. Babbitt (1828-1905) wrote a book entitled "The Principals of Light and Colour; The Classical Study of the Healing Power of Colour". In this book he reveals the relationships between colour healing, sound and rhythm on humans and plants. Edwin developed solarized (Sun infused) waters using coloured lenses as filters. Edwin claimed the "potentised" water retained the necessary elements and energies of each particular colour and achieved spectacular results in his healing sessions.

"Sunlight is the principal curative agent in nature's laboratory and where light cannot enter, disease does". *Dr. Edwin D. Babbitt*

Dinshaw Ghadiali (1873-1966) wrote "Let There Be Light", in which he describes his Spectro-Chrome Color Therapy using Colour and light to heal illness.

Between 1924 and 1958, the AMA and the FDA were obsessed with going after Dinshaw, attempting to brand him as a charlatan, whose machine and research was simply useless. Oddly enough, Dinshaws Spectro-Chrome Therapy machine was used quite successfully in a hospital in Pennsylvania, as well as having been used by hundreds of medical professionals. Even during the plague years of the early 1900's, Dinshaws "unorthodox" practices affected 60 per cent of those treated with colour, as opposed to 40 percent by means of conventional medicine.

It was because of the AMA and the FDA trying for years to shut him down, that Dinshaw took a slight detour and took his Spectro-Chrome Therapy to a different level…a level the AMA, nor the FDA could touch.

In 1933, Dinshaw developed a complete home study course entitled "Spectro-Chrom Metry". In this wonderfully detailed book Dinshaw shows how to heal many ailments, illnesses and diseases by applying particular colours to various points on the body similar to acupressure and acupuncture points. He won the battle and was not sought after by the AMA or the FDA anymore. The fourth edition was published in 1997.

"Truth can be defeated, never conquered." *Darius Dinshaw Ghadiali*

Dr. Neils Finsen (1860-1904) of Denmark first publicized the effects of using coloured light onTuberculosis. By using light to stimulate the brain, Dr. Finsen found improvement within the physical, emotional and mental states.

With colour and light, he successfully treated restriction of field vision, short attention span, hypersensitivity to bright lights, and problems with focusing. In 1896, Dr. Finsen founded what is now called the "Finsen Institute of Copenhagen", and in 1903, Dr. Neils Finsen won a Nobel Prize for his work on the use of light on disease.

Vicky Wall (1918-1991) was a visionary, an alchemist, an apothecary of extraordinary measures, and the founder and creator of Aura-Soma Therapy. She wrote a book entitled "The Miracle of Colour Healing, Aura-Soma Therapy as the Mirror of the Soul".

In her book she describes how she was guided in meditation to make the first series of colourful "Balance" bottles containing remarkable healing powers, even though she had lost her sight. Vicky was born in England, the seventh child of a seventh child, and possessed a wealth of knowledge regarding plants and herbs, as well as the mysteries of the Universe itself.

Without Vicky, many of us, including myself, would not be around to teach the magick of colour therapy and the mysticism behind it. We would not be able to witness or experience the miracles of the "quantum" shifts of consciousness and release of physical pain on ourselves as well as our clients/patients while using such magickal frequencies. Vicky listened to her guidance, trusted it and "stepped off the edge" to create something which is inevitably changing the world of healing. Vicky was a "true" mystic, a visionary and pioneer.

Theo Gimbel, is known as one of Britain's leading experts on colour therapy, and is the author of two books entitled "Healing through Colour" and "Healing with Colour and

Light". He continued the work of Rudolph Steiner, and established the Hygeia Studios and College of Color Therapy in Britain.

Theo, through his research and practice discovered that through the energies of light and sound, illness could be balanced, therefore healed. With the appropriate colour and sound being delivered into the proper channels within the body, negative patterns and emotions which when built up and not dealt with can cause disease, can be diffused to create a harmonious state within the physical, emotional and mental bodies.

"As a result of the slightest change, either voluntary or involuntary, the aura patterns dance and vibrate, change colour to some extent and reflect all that goes on in a person". *Theo Gimbel*

Chapter VI

With the Birth of Christianity Came the "Dark Ages"

"Where there is light, there is no darkness, where there is darkness there is no light".
Carl Jung

350 – 500 AD marked the Middle Ages also referred to as the "Dark Ages". During this time, those who practiced the Pagan way of life were banished or persecuted. This also included the banishing of any healing practices of the Egyptians, Greeks and Romans, which used the natural forces of the Universe.

In 391 AD the Christians destroyed the temple of Serapis at Alexandria which housed one of the world's greatest libraries and said to have had over half a million scrolls. The scrolls spoke of the magick and mysticism of the Universe. What happened to the Pagan libraries in Greece and Rome? It was common for the Roman Emperors to commission public libraries often attached to temples. Even the Roman schools, colleges and public baths had libraries. So, why were the Christians so fearful of the information contained in all of these writings? Could it have been, and possibly still be, that they feared something greater and more powerful than themselves existed in the Universe? They did not have the "real" faith it required to know that everything is as it should be, that all is in Divine Order, and there is no need for control or manipulation of others. If one comes from a place of lack of power within, living a fearful life, it is considered to be a place of weakness. The need to control or manipulate on any level would be done so out of fear, thus fear is the shadow, and darkness itself.

During the rise of Christianity in Europe, those who continued to practice the ancient ways of the healing arts through colour and light were forced to do it in secrecy. To maintain honor within the Hermetic teachings, the magick was well guarded from the abusive hands of the public by the temple priests, some of who gladly gave their lives to keep the practice of this "high magick" in silence. It was the exclusive domain of Royalty, priests and Initiates. These sacred arts were passed on to Initiates via secret oral tradition to continue the line of knowledge, as well as in the legacy of symbols and hieroglyphs left behind in the great temples of Egypt to empower the mind of the seeker.

It is the temples themselves, which are the teachings. It is they, through their very structures that help us to "re-member" who we are and where we come from. It is through the sophistication of the symbolism, that the seeker, on a higher conscious level, is shown how to understand the transformational process through archetypal energies.

This is esoteric wisdom in art form and vibration, a component of magickal technology, showing the soul how to develop wisdom of the Heart, thereby transforming itself. According to John Anthony West, an extraordinary Egyptologist and mystic symbolist, it is the temples, which evoke in us a sense of the eternal, the Divine, the sacred.

"Hieroglyphs are the principals of the transformation of the soul anchored by visible symbols." *Magical Egypt DVD series*

"Symbolism is the first veil of the language of magick." *Magical Egypt DVD series*

"Egypt is the keeper of secrets, the land of riddles, the birthplace of magick, and the home of the mystery schools." *Magical Egypt DVD series*

It was the Ancient Egyptians, Greeks and Roman Pagans who worshipped the Sun, or in metaphor, "the light". Yet, the moment Christianity came into play, it became one of the darkest moments in the history of humanity. This resulted in more bloodshed then, and still continues now in the "name of God", righteousness and false ego. This is an example of human Will against Divine Will.

Where was the "light" in forcing people to believe what was not in their Hearts, or to worship something they did not believe in? Where was the "light" in the judgment and intolerance of those people who hurt no one, yet because of their belief systems which were different and did not conform like the masses, were murdered in the name of God? Just what kind of a God would dictate murder? Where was the so-called "light" when Christianity came in? Did not Jesus teach of compassion, tolerance and unconditional love? Or, was this too, stricken and left out "conveniently" by the Christians as they re-wrote their books to control the masses?

Without light it became a dark consciousness, literally the "Dark Ages". All forms of light and colour healing were banned from use. All "politicians" in the church knew that if the masses could take responsibility for their own well- being and talk to God themselves to get answers, excluding the church as a "middleman", that they would not need them to dictate how to live, walk, talk, nor could they tell them what to believe in. The "flock" mentality would not exist. This would mean the end of the church, which they feared and still fear most today.

Suppress the masses by keeping them in fear, control their belief systems by altering the bible (which by the way was written by man) and tell them they are all born into damnation and unworthiness. Thus, keep them weak with fear…KEEP THEM IN THE DARK.

The Dark Ages came as a result of those who tried to control the masses out of their own fears of inadequacy and greed. The result of removing "light" from daily life was over one third the population of Europe dying from diseases…diseases, which needed the "light" to be healed.

Hmmm, something to think about.

Chapter VII

The Emerald Tablets

Over the past several thousand years, it has been discovered by some of the greatest minds in history that as light beings, we need light frequencies to heal. The original church fathers based their teachings and belief systems upon the writings in the *"Emerald Tablets"*, 17 Emerald Tablets based on the writings upon a single Emerald Tablet known collectively as the *Corpus Hermetico*. The Tablets were brought forth by Thoth the Atlantean, also known as Tehuti(Djehuti), meaning "Truth" and "Time". Thoth was known as the first Hermes, previously mentioned in Chapter III.

Amenhotep IV, also known as Ahkenaten, was considered the second Hermes who continued the enlightened teachings during his rule from 1364-1347 B.C.E.

He was the only Pharaoh in history who changed Egyptian worship from many Gods to the one God, the Aten meaning the "disk", creating a monotheistic religion which recognized the visible Sun as the source of all creative energy...the "light".

The third Hermes, a man named Balinas and later being known as *Apollonius of Tyana*, was named after the great healing God Apollo. His life will be explored later on in the book.

In Greek Mythology, Hermes is the Messenger of the Gods. Here we have three separate Hermes' in ancient history who, were here to bring into human consciousness the possibilities of enlightenment through the transformation of the soul, i.e. messages from the Divine.

The *"Emerald Tablets"* are thought to go back to the dawn of time. They have been called many names, but there is one that stands out beyond the rest that is known throughout the world and most assuredly amongst all alchemists and wizards in present day. It is called "The Philosophers Stone".

So legend says, the *"Emerald Tablets"* were first discovered by the young Greek King, Alexander the Great, born in 356 B.C. in Pella, Macedonia in the shadow of Mount Olympus...home of the Gods.

In 332 B.C.E., Alexander had conquered Syria and had become Pharaoh, also inheriting all treasures of Egypt, including the *"Emerald Tablets"*, which lay in Hermes' Tomb.

In the winter of that same year, Alexander journeyed to Siwa in the Libyan Desert to see the Oracle of Ammon (Ammon is Zeus to the Greeks) seeking signs from the Gods. He did not want to displease them and fall out of favor before making his next journey to seek out the *"Emerald Tablets"*, as well as to further his quest to conquer all of Asia. Heracles (Hercules to the Romans) and Perseus, legendary ancestors of Alexander's, were also said to have visited the Oracle.

Alexander discovered the tomb just east of Siwa, a nine day journey from the Nile.

It contained the most beautiful jeweled Egyptian statues, Hermes' Golden throne displaying his mummified corpse, numerous stacks of scrolls written by the hand of Hermes, and of course, the *"Emerald Tablets"*... magickal visions of light to which was said nothing else compared.

After his discovery of the tomb, Alexander had the Tablets and all the contents of the tomb transported to Memphis, then to Heliopolis. Shortly after Alexander's arrival in Heliopolis, he ordered the construction of the great Alexandrian Library to house and study the Hermetic scrolls written by the hands of Thoth, the first Hermes. These scrolls, at that time, were thought to have been 9000 years old...possibly older.

A scribe known as Manetho, meaning "Gift of Thoth", was brought to Egypt from Greece to translate the writings of Thoth into Greek, as they were written in an ancient Phoenician alphabet. Apparently he recorded his findings, which were much greater than he had expected. In his translations he found the secret placements of the original texts placed in two locations, inside a pillar in Heliopolis and one in Thebes, thought now to be over 13,000 years old.

As acknowledged in the Egyptian holy books, these "Pillars of the Gods of the Dawning Light" were later moved to a third temple in Phoenicia known as the "Pillars of Hermes". They were described by Herodotus as such; "One pillar was of pure Gold, and the other was of Emerald, which glowed at night with great brilliancy".

Solon, the famous Greek statesman, legislator and grandfather to Plato saw the tablets and wrote of their contents, which memorialized the destruction of Atlantis.

Alexander, having access to this type of esoteric information and not having had many decades of required teachings and disciplines as the temple priests and other famous figures such as Plato and Pythagoras, was like a child opening Pandora's Box, not realizing its power. One must have wisdom of the Heart to wield such knowledge, and a disciplined spiritual background to harness its energies.

It was noted by Alexander's companions and those who traveled with him that after Alexander spent much time with the *Emerald Tablets* in Siwa, his personality began to change...and not for the better. Even though Alexander was declared a God and a son of Zeus by the Oracle of Siwa, known to the Egyptians as *"Ammon Ra"*, and had access to the teachings from the *Emerald Tablets* to show him how to transform into a "God-like" being, his ego got the better of him. He began thinking of himself as a God, demanding that everyone treated him like one, Persian style. He wore Royal Persian clothes, ate Persian food, and lived the Persian lifestyle. This did not sit well with his Macedonian generals, nor any other Greeks. This resulted in many attempts on his life by his Royal pages, all of which were betrayed and tortured to death.

Alexander's mother, Olympias, played an extremely large roll in his growing ego from the time he was a child. She was a woman of great vision, power and control, and did everything she could for him. This included having many people murdered who might be a threat to her son. In her eyes she did what any mother would do ...and that was to make sure that Alexander was always in a position of power while away from his kingdom, conquering the world.

Interestingly enough, Alexander was mentioned in the Holy Koran as being a God. Archangel Gabriel's message in Revelations to the Prophet Mohammad says, "We established his power on Earth and we gave him the ways and means to all ends". Was he a God? …who knows? One thing is for sure; to the Persians, Alexander was a tyrant, and the Devil himself.

According to Plutarch, a famous Greek historian born in AD 46, on Alexander's way to Babylon, Chaldean Priests prophesied his death should he enter the city. Alexander ignored their warnings. It is said "bad omens" began shortly there after.

As he approached the city walls, he saw several crows fighting with each other, some falling dead where he stood. Other omens were to follow. He found an ordinary man sitting on his throne in a trance, and his largest and most powerful lion was kicked to death by a donkey. The omens became so frequent and ominous that Alexander became frightened, as he felt he had fallen out of favor with the Gods.

Regardless, Alexander entered the city gates of Babylon with the strength of a lion. When he arrived, he apparently indulged himself in heavy drinking at the many banquets he attended. One night he went too far.

Because he died suddenly, speculation is that the twelve pints of wine he consumed that night were poisoned, or possibly it was the toll his body had taken from becoming an alcoholic after the death of his long time lover and companion, Hephaestion, the year prior. Alexander's grief consumed him. He was Heartbroken and played out his pain through acts of rage and many drinking excursions. He crucified the doctor who treated Hephaestion, and ordered all the manes and tails of the animals in his army to be cut off as a sign of mourning. He also banned all music, then proceeded into the country of the Cossaeans, just northeast of Babylon. There he acted out his rage by massacring the entire nation. He had no justification for the murder of so many. This was called a sacrifice to Hephaestion's ghost. Today, it would be called a war crime.

In the summer of 323 B.C., after attending a drinking party thrown by his friend Medios of Larisa, Alexander fell into an illness plagued by fever, chills, abdominal pain and a slow onset of paralysis (most probably it was typhoid fever), gradually becoming worse over the following 10 days. On the 11th day, June 10th, Alexander slipped into a coma and died. He was only 32.

The son of God or the devil himself, leader or tyrant…it was his path, and he fulfilled it with great courage, strength, and most of all, pain. Today, he is still remembered as one of the greatest generals that ever lived, and certainly, he was the youngest.

Three hundred years later, Balinas, a young boy born in the year 4 B.C in Tyana, (Cappadocia) Turkey, picked up where Alexander left off. From the time of his birth, he was destined to change the course of human history for almost two thousand years. Even his birth date was the same acknowledged year as Jesus, and they seemingly traveled the same lands and received similar educations, becoming Initiates of the Ancient Temples in Egypt and Greece. Balinas was known not only for his beauty, but also his ability to speak every human language without having been learned in any of them. Many believed that it was Balinas, later known as Apollonius of Tyana, who really was Jesus Christ. The Delphi Oracle proclaimed him to be yet another son of Zeus, as She did Alexander the Great.

Prior to his birth, it was prophesied that he would be the incarnation of Proteus the Greek sea God and Shepard of the ocean, who was filled with great wisdom and said to know all things past, present and future. Because he did not like to speak his prophesies, he was known for shape shifting at will, as to not be recognized. If he were caught, he would have to give the seeker an answer to a question. However, he was known for defying all capture.

It was Balinas who rediscovered Alexander's hiding place for the *Emerald Tablets* just outside of Tyana in 32 C.E. The tablets on the monument were written in the original Syrian alphabet. One which lay on it had the following message: "Behold! I am Hermes Trismegistus, he who is threefold in wisdom. I once placed these marvelous signs openly before all eyes; but now I have veiled them by my wisdom, so that none should attain them unless he become a sage like myself." A breastplate further up read. "Let him who would learn and know the secrets of creation and nature inquire beneath my feet." For many a night, Balinas went to this beautiful statue, sat at the feet of Hermes and conversed with him as if he were alive.

When Balinas was fourteen, frustrated and upset by his mystical studies, his parents sent him to Tarsus to learn from a Phoenician teacher named Euthydemus, to continue a more formal education. Balinas became so upset with the "frivolousness" of the Tarsians that he convinced his father to allow him to move to the Aegae and take up quarters with his master Euxenes, to pursue studies at a temple of Aesclepius. There he discovered the teachings of Hermes through the writings of Pythagoras, who was said to be a direct descendent of Hermes himself. This is where Balinas's gifts of healing and clairvoyance became known.

For the next two years he was taught by the priests and doctors who healed by the laying on of hands and by the wielding energies of the unseen. They practiced magick and the art of interpreting dreams. As mentioned in Chapter IV, pilgrimages were made from all over Greece, Syria, and Alexandria for consultations with the priests.

At the age of sixteen, Balinas returned to Tyana to complete his apprenticeship with the marble statue he'd come to know so well. The "light" went on when Balinas read the words inscribed on the breastplate once again, "Let him who would learn and know the secrets of creation and nature, inquire beneath my feet." Taking the message literally, Balinas realized that the tomb was below the statue. He began digging under the stone block until the entrance to the chamber was revealed. Hearing a "guiding voice", Balinas was instructed to make a lantern of sorts by putting a torch within a glass vessel. He entered the dark chamber below and discovered the *Emerald Tablet* resting in Hermes' tomb. The Tablet glowed ominously in the candlelight.

As he carefully moved about the chamber, he stumbled over a pile of books lying on Hermes' feet. Four of these books were written by the hand of Hermes. Balinas carefully opened them up. He discovered that written in the first three books were advanced instruction on astronomy and mathematics. On the fourth book was written the following inscription: "This is the secret of the creation and the knowledge of the causes of all things."

For several months Balinas returned to the cave to study the books with complete openness of the mind and Heart. Shortly after, he took a vow of silence for five years, before journeying further into the outside world, only communicating through his eyes and other physical gestures. He renounced all worldly goods, the killing of animals for ritual sacrifice, wore only linen garments, shoes made of tree bark, and became a strict vegetarian. By the age of twenty-one, Balinas knew it was time to venture into the world to spread the enlightened teachings of Hermes. Historians documented his travels throughout Greece, Persia, Egypt, India, North Africa, Spain, and other European countries as well.

During his travels, Balinas was disheartened to learn that many religious sects had forgotten their connection to the Divine, having become materialistic in the process. Balinas was there to reestablish that connection for whoever would listen. He instructed the priests in their temples and shrines of the Hermetic Mysteries of what is hidden and unseen to help them understand the art of spiritual realization.

Before parting, he would always leave a talisman made of metal or gemstones charged with his spiritual energy, or his "light", to ensure the spirituality of those who came within its presence, and even those who did not.

At this time, Balinas became known as Apollonius to the world. He received Divine honors wherever he went. His level of clairvoyance was astounding, and his predictions came to pass.

Around 70 C.E., the city of Alexandria became Apollonius's center of operations, and is said to have written most of his books there. The most famous is entitled, "The Book of Balinas the Wise on Causes", which contained the writings of the *Emerald Tablets*. This later became known in Europe as the *Book of the Secrets of Creation*.

Before Apollonius died in 98 C.E., he spoke these words to a close friend: "Whenever you think on high matters in solitary meditation, you will find me."

He was over eighty years old.

Strangely enough, Apollonius's body was never found after he died. Could it be that he did indeed practice the magick he learned as a Pythagorean Initiate? Did Apollonius utilize this ancient practice and perform a miracle at his own death? Did he actually transform into the "Philosophers Stone"? Quite possibly he did. He was, after all, a mystic and a magician. And, what of Pythagoras? There are no known tombs anywhere for either Apollonius or Pythagoras. Interesting.

In 120 CE, 23 years after Roman Emperor Hadrian's death, The Emerald Tablet was acquired for his personal library. Where it went from there…nobody knows.

Chapter VIII

Alchemy and the Materia Prima

The word *Alchemy* is thought to come from "Khemet", the Arabic word for Egypt. "Al-Khemet" means "from the Black Lands". In the *Emerald Tablets*, tablet V, Thoth (Hermes) speaks of bringing his wisdom and magick from Atlantis to the children of Khem. The Greek translation offers the following: Kmt/Kemet meaning the word "Egypt" and Khymeia, meaning "the Black". This is possibly describing the art of treating or the transformation of "Black metal" to produce precious metals. Another translation for Khymeia is "fusion", or the melting of Silver and Gold.

The process of transforming coal into diamonds and Black metals into Gold is the same process the soul journeys through, and the end results will be from choices made by the soul. In other words it is the choice we make as souls as to how we will procure our path in this world. Will we stay in density and unhealthy thoughts, or "coal", causing a life of suffering and pain, or will we choose to ascend to the light, or the "diamond", by listening to guidance from "out of the Blue", i.e. the Heavens.

In Egypt during the year of 296 AD, according to Byzantine history, the Roman Emperor Diocletian had all documents and the formulations with use of "Khymeia" or alchemical recipes they contained destroyed. This act of destruction was implemented with the intent of controlling all information being viewed by the public, which would allow anyone reading these documents to understand that the power of change lies within themselves. This would give less power to the Roman Empire and the churches as also stated in Chapter VI.

What was Diocletian afraid of? **He was afraid of losing power.**

As mentioned before, many attempts were made to destroy all teachings of alchemy by those seeking to control the thoughts of mankind. The secrets have continued to be passed from one generation to the next via secret societies and mystic symbols shrouded in allegory and hidden meaning. This ancient knowledge has acquired a life force of its own and continues to re-emerge into the consciousness of man, much like the Phoenix out of its own ashes.

Materia Prima, or "First Matter", is also referred to as the "Fifth Element", the quintessence, and the matter in which the Heavens are made of. The Materia Prima is composed of all things, energies, elements (air, fire, water, earth), negatives and positives, vegetable, mineral, plant and animal. The Materia Prima is the Moon and the Sun, fire and ice, health and disease, descending into destruction and ascending again back into illumination. The Materia Prima is all, and is the primordial source of creation itself. This is the energy from which alchemy is based.

As mentioned in Chapter VII, *"The Emerald Tablets"* contain mystical instruction of the seven alchemical steps the soul must take to transform itself to a higher level of consciousness. Each step must be completed before taking the next. It is very much like an initiation process. For example, in life, many of us go to school, take tests, etc. Life is the same. We are constantly faced with challenges that test us and push us out of the box and beyond our comfort zone to see if we'll pass them. They too, are initiation tests the Universe gives us to see if we are ready to move to higher levels.

According to the Ancient Egyptians, it is the Ka (soul/spirit/ air) that has a choice as to how it will fulfill its destiny. All humans are born with a purpose and gifts to procure that purpose. It is up to us whether we walk that path or not.

The path we choose is paved by our conscious thoughts, which are influenced by external forces. If a low road is chosen, there will be constant suffering in life, as in death. To choose a higher road will help the soul accelerate and move easily into other worlds. Were the Egyptians right? Did they know the answer to something thousands of years ago we now seek today?

In the DVD series of *"Magical Egypt"* by John Anthony West and Chance Gardner, they refer to the Egyptian practice of *"The Materia Prima of Consciousness"*. According to their research, this consists of our attention, our awareness, our individuality, our inspiration, and our intellect, utilizing these elements to bring our consciousness into higher states of being.

The same laws that govern transformation of the outer worlds also apply to the transformation of the inner soul, as mentioned previously in the beginning of the chapter. It is the same process to turn lower base materials (darker, denser energies) to higher states of illumination such as coal into diamonds and base metals into Gold.

If our "Ka", or soul, chooses to remain in a lower state such as charcoal or lower base metals with too much attachment to the outer or material world, we will remain fragile and can easily be broken down. To remain in a "chaotic", or unclear state of mind, our reactions to traumatic situations will follow suit as such, thus not allowing resolve on any level, nor any kind of healing to take place.

For example; Be it involvement in an accident, injury to a loved one, or even a natural disaster, it is only when we are able to shift out of emotionally unstable and hysterical responses to the situation that we can move into a serene and peaceful state of mind. This allows us to focus, so we are more likely to find resolve, help, and healing to these types of situations. We must remember to constantly shift out of the "coal" state of mind, so we may live each day in the "illumination" of a diamond, for when light is shed upon chaotic moments, all answers will come with Divine guidance.

In metaphor within our soul we experience, "Divide and conquer". This means if our physical, emotional, mental and spiritual states of being are not aligned or properly nurtured, and indeed out of sorts or divided, this can lead to fragility creating illness and disease.

However, should we recognize our many levels of consciousness and how to align with their complexities, it then becomes possible to work with Universal powers given to us to maximize the potential of sculpting a diamond out of ourselves, for a diamond is beautiful, luminous and impenetrable. Yet, a diamond is used to cut through foreign objects with great precision. Could this, in fact, be a metaphor for our journey in this world, continuously being tested by the Universe, having to cut through what no longer serves our higher purpose, creating feelings of "lightness" or "illumination" within our souls? Are we truly being moved up "Jacobs Ladder"? Perhaps. Thus, it would make sense that the extraordinary qualities we seek to carry within ourselves of integrity, self-love, self-worth and self-esteem, courage, and reverence, are but a few qualities in our quest for enlightenment, necessary to feel impenetrable… like the diamond.

Comparative Maps of Egypt

Ancient Egypt

Modern Egypt

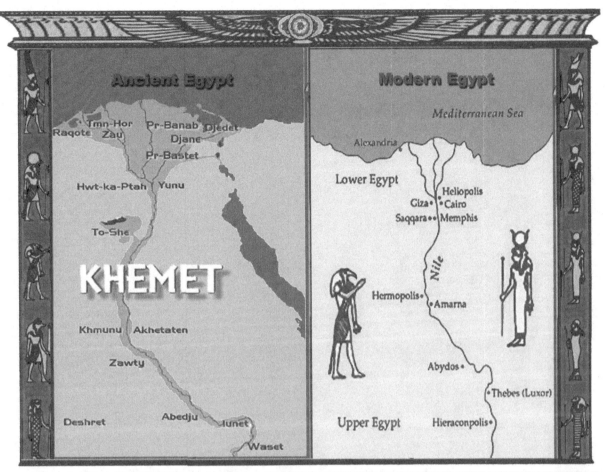

Illustration of Spiritual Alchemy

Spiritual Alchemy: The Seven Levels

of Transformation and How

They Relate to

The Soul

Spiritual Alchemy:
The Seven Levels of Transformation
of the Soul and How
They Relate to the Chakras

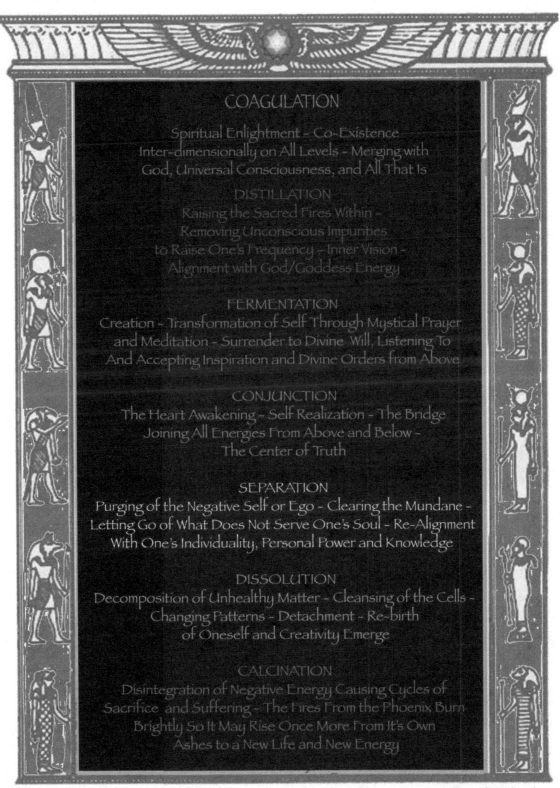

COAGULATION

Spiritual Enlightment - Co-Existence
Inter-dimensionally on All Levels - Merging with
God, Universal Consciousness, and All That Is

DISTILLATION

Raising the Sacred Fires Within -
Removing Unconscious Impurities
to Raise One's Frequency - Inner Vision -
Alignment with God/Goddess Energy

FERMENTATION

Creation - Transformation of Self Through Mystical Prayer
and Meditation - Surrender to Divine Will, Listening To
And Accepting Inspiration and Divine Orders from Above

CONJUNCTION

The Heart Awakening - Self Realization - The Bridge
Joining All Energies From Above and Below -
The Center of Truth

SEPARATION

Purging of the Negative Self or Ego - Clearing the Mundane -
Letting Go of What Does Not Serve One's Soul - Re-Alignment
With One's Individuality, Personal Power and Knowledge

DISSOLUTION

Decomposition of Unhealthy Matter - Cleansing of the Cells -
Changing Patterns - Detachment - Re-birth
of Oneself and Creativity Emerge

CALCINATION

Disintegration of Negative Energy Causing Cycles of
Sacrifice and Suffering - The Fires From the Phoenix Burn
Brightly So It May Rise Once More From It's Own
Ashes to a New Life and New Energy

Chapter IX

Awakening the Soul Through the Ancient Wisdom of Colour

Colour therapy has been shown to us in many forms by some of the most famous hermeticists in the ancient and modern world. Masterminds of their time, they provided the world with documents going back over thousands of years. Their writings show that light, containing all colours and frequencies, as well as other forms of colour therapies, could help people heal all types of ailments including chronic diseases. We've experienced much of these teachings through preserved documents of the ancient world as well as in writings of present time.

It is the *"Materia Prima"*, meaning it is our consciousness we must utilize to bring us to the next step of our souls transformation. It is the seven levels of alchemy that we must walk through to perfect our souls, should we choose. It is the same in life as in metaphor for turning lead into Gold or "heaviness into light", coal into a diamond, or "darkness into light". It is alchemy of the soul in its purest form.

If we choose to accept this sacred marriage between science and spirit, we indeed can learn the magickal art of the transformation of the soul. Truly listening to the chords we play within can prevent "discord" in our daily lives, possibly preventing illness and disease.

By using colour, it can help remove our darkness, literally bringing things to "light", exposing what does not serve us anymore so we can go on with our lives with an awakened consciousness, thus moving to much higher levels spiritually.

To bring ourselves into the ultimate state of happiness and bliss we must let go of that which causes any negative or heavy energies in our lives. This is why it is called "enlightenment". The moment the light enters the Heart allowing the truth to be heard, the physical body becomes lighter because the vibration level has been raised. It is the soul finally responding to the orders being issued from above via many dimensions of loving and compassionate beings who love us more than we could ever love ourselves.

Love is the frequency we are so desperately missing, and yet, is the very frequency that is held for us by the Universe hoping that one day we will recognize loves arrival, and allow our Hearts to open up and reach back.

Keeping our Hearts open to all possibilities will allow the Universe to present all possibilities to us. It is how we respond to the guidance that will make the difference between our lives being in "order" or in "chaos".

This is the legacy of mysticism and high magick left to us by the Universe brought forth to humanity in ancient writings. It is a very large multidimensional book that has been broken down by many Masters over many centuries, hoping that each time we would get closer to the truth.

Opening this ancient book of wisdom will change all who embrace its magickal teachings.

Are you ready?

Chapter X

The Modern Day Quest for Truth

I have acknowledged John Anthony West throughout this book as an extraordinary Egyptologist/Symbolist/Pythagorean/Scholar/Writer. He wrote an explorative work of art with "Serpent in the Sky: The High Wisdom of Ancient Egypt", in which he turned the entire world of Egyptology upside down. John presented symbolist interpretations through the work of R.A. Schwaller de Lubicz, regarding temples, statues, Pharaohs and the mysticism the Egyptians learned in the Mystery Schools which elevated their levels of consciousness to places of bliss and enlightenment.

John is one of only a few who has continued the masterful work of R.A. Schwaller de Lubicz (1891-1962), who was a French scholar, symbolist and philosopher that spent fifteen years at the Temple of Luxor. While there, R.A. Schwaller de Lubicz discovered and published his findings in several books *(The Temple of Man, Symbol and the Symbolic, Sacred Science)* regarding the spiritual and cosmological insights of the Ancient Egyptians. He took Egyptology beyond orthodox thinking, which according to John Anthony West has not been very well disproved to this day by conventional Egyptologists.

The very people claiming to be "legitimate" Egyptologists, are the very same people who are not willing to step "out of the box" in their thinking, possibly covering up evidence for ego sake, and most certainly...not wanting to rock the boat.

In 1993, John won an Emmy for his insightful research in *"Mystery of the Sphinx"*, hosted by Charlton Heston. His latest DVD series, *"Magical Egypt"*, is phenomenal in my opinion, taking the mind of the watcher into an alternative place of thought using "out of the box" interpretations, helping one understand the science of the unseen, and what lies beyond the veil of our consciousness. John Anthony West shows how these symbols left behind by the Ancient Egyptians may help us to understand and even heal ourselves through learning techniques to help us transform our souls into a higher state of being.

It is important to understand Ancient Egypt and the Ancient Egyptians through the minds of the visionaries like R.A. Schwaller de Lubicz and John Anthony West, who show us other possibilities through the very artifacts left behind as learning devices by the ancients themselves. Colour therapy, sound and light were key factors in the healing, acceleration and transformation of the soul. All modalities aforementioned assisted the Ancient Egyptians in the development of the "Intelligence of the Heart", aligning them with the laws of creation.

In colour therapy, the intelligence of the Heart represents the colours Yellow (intelligence/mental energy) and Green (Heart/truth/feeling energy). The meaning is simple...do you listen to your Heart and know when it's energy opens, thus your life flows easily, or do you constantly make choices that go against your instincts by rationalizing in your mind, thus ending up in a lesson of betrayal...your betrayal.

Simply put, are you on your path, or off your path…only your Heart holds your truth.

That is the "Intelligence of the Heart".

Testimonials

Leslie,

Where do I start? My journey to healing had been underway for some time when we met for the first time. My childhood held all the wonderful memories & experiences that a childhood should hold. However, it also held some horrific experiences which threatened to paralyze me with fears yet again if I didn't grab hold & face them head on with FAITH in the lessons I had to learn & HOPE for the love I could share as I moved through them.

I had been doing just that for approximately 12 years. About half way through my journey, we met…and you helped me find hope & get in touch with the beautiful little girl inside me, the one whom I had lost along the way. Then, 6 years, one amazing marriage, and two Miracle children later, we sat across from each other and you spoke the words…"It's Time…"

With tears in my eyes, we began our session later that day. I saw the beautiful bottles and the amazing colors….my Heart led me to the ones I needed, and I remember how wonderfully taken care of I felt…in that moment. Then, as the healing session began, I immediately felt transformed. Having never worked with the bottles, I didn't know what to expect….the energy & love that comes as they lay over you, and the light coming through….your amazing energy & the channeling of Angels all around….it was a LIFE CHANGING experience.

The emotions were wonderfully overwhelming & my Heart is so full upon recalling what happened. I can only sum it up by saying that when we were finished, feeling the Angels & Spirits surrounding us with Love, Light & Protection, I muttered two words that I had hoped I would be able to say one day…."IT'S OVER!"

It was like we were able to unlock a door, that up until this point was still closed to me: a door that took me one step closer to the me I really wanted to be…the me who'd never been hurt. It seemed to culminate the healing work that I had done up until that point, taking off one of the "last layers", if you will.

The magickal thing is that through this experience, it reminded me again how we're all here to help one another…and that all I'd been through was ultimately to help me help others as well. Our work has helped me feel safe & secure enough to do that.

Thank you Leslie for using your gifts to help me. Thank you for helping me connect even further with the Love & Light that is within us all!

P.S.
Oh yes, I would be remiss if I didn't mention the amazing work Leslie did with our 3 1/2 year old son. When he was 7 months old, he underwent some tests, for what fortunately turned out to be nothing. However, one of them required he be put under. Upon his awakening, we were with the doctor and couldn't be found for about 20 minutes. When we finally got to him, he was quite upset and it took us some time to comfort him.

Later on in his life, he kept awakening with episodes of crying, which I immediately recognized from that moment when he was a baby. He told us he felt alone, like when he was in the hospital. We had been comforting him, praying with him and reminding him that he was never alone. I just had a feeling that if Leslie could work with him, it would seal the deal!

She came over, brought the colours and "played" with him for about 15 minutes. From that night on, the cry is gone! He just loves his protective dragons who give him courage in the Royal Magenta Bottle he has. He loves to run through the "magickal mist" when I spray it. It makes him feel safe.

H.J.

Leslie,

When I first came to you I had a devastating immune disorder called shingles, and I was in so much pain that I couldn't get up on your treatment table by myself, and my left eye was completely red, swollen and closed.

During the session with the colours I had chosen, I saw angels around me, and I also saw myself in Heaven surrounded by other angels. This was something I will never forget. As you were working on me with the colours and lights, at one point I felt a force of energy moving through my Heart, pulling pain out, so much I had to open my eyes, yet, you weren't there. I thought you moved the bottle over me, which later you told me was Illumination Turquoise, and you had actually worked with it about ten minutes prior. When I opened my eyes to see what was happening, the bottle was resting above the right side of my Heart. You hadn't touched it. Then I began to cry. As I cried I knew I was releasing pain, pain I held in my Heart for so long. It was this pain I buried which caused my illness. It was the words you spoke, and the magic within the colours which brought this realization to "light".

After the session was over, I jumped back up on the table so you could show me how to use my bottles at home, and I realized I had no more pain, and my left eye had opened slightly.

I went home and slept like I've not slept in three months because of the extreme pain I've been living with.

Six months after my treatment, I had an awakening experience, which you spoke of in my session. My life has completely taken a turn into the light, I am free and I feel beautiful.

You are so amazing, for what you did for me. Your words and colours helped me to heal so much in one session, and since then doors have opened up, allowing me to sort everything out in my life. You helped me to see with "clear eyes" what was really happening to me. Because of this, my eyes healed as well.

I keep my bottles on my dresser and I feel a special angelic relationship with them. This experience has helped me to heal on so many levels, especially with my physical and emotional pain. I didn't think I could get through this, yet it was through this very deep conscious shift that I finally realized myself.

I feel so blessed to know you.

Thank you Leslie.

Rosaura Zapata

Where do I begin to explain the phenomenal experiences I have had, with *Auracle's Colour Therapy Bottles*…

To try to put in words the incredible shifts I have experienced in my body, in my Heart and in my life when working with the Colours is like trying to explain God. For what

I have had the blessing to witness first hand with the Colours is so personal and yet so monumental in my own healing that I want to share this experience with as many people as I can.

I have had many un-expected experiences with the Colours, and it is in these experiences that I have come to absolutely believe in their power to heal combined with the desire to heal with absolute conviction. When working with the Colours, I have seen physical changes in my body take place; watching the release of old scar tissue dissolve, feeling my Heart opening at an incredible pace, seeing the Angelic presence more clearly over me while the Colours are on my body, as well as witnessing past pain(s) release from my Heart and experiencing a complete physical release.

Most recently while my husband and I were trying to conceive our first child we were informed from the Western Medical community that we had a 5% chance of becoming pregnant. It was Leslie's work with both my husband and myself and the Colours that I truly believe allowed us a miracle of our current pregnancy.

Leslie is a remarkable and Extraordinary gifted healer who has spent years of research, time, energy and love to bring to life a beautiful healing modality that is designed to penetrate deep into the Heart and allow shifts to begin.

In my opinion, there is no other product on the market today that has the amount of research, pure ingredients, and devotion to love than Auracle's Colour Therapy Bottles.

My life is forever changed from the Colours and what Leslie has created for all of us to remain on our path to self-love.

Denise Bella Vlasis-Gascon

Index of Terms

Acupuncture – An Eastern based treatment of pain or disease whereby the tips of fine needles are inserted into specific points or meridians on the body.

Angels - Benevolent and loving celestial beings who act as an intermediary between Heaven and Earth.

Archangels – A hierarchy of Angelic beings who are overseers of different angelic realms, giving special instructions to be carried out for the healing of humanity.

Archetype – An unseen force or energy, a pattern from which behaviors are modeled i.e. the Goddess, Queen, Healer, Faerie, Victim, Miser, Teacher, Scholar, King, Artist, etc.

Ascended Masters – An enlightened teacher who walked the earth as a human, and continues to guide humanity from the heavens.

Aura – A field of electrical energy which surrounds every living organism.

Chakras – Seven wheels of energy or light connected into our spinal column, which effect our consciousness, physically, emotionally, mentally and spiritually.

Chi – Life force (see Meridians)

Consciousness – Self- realization, an understanding of self-mastery on the physical, emotional, mental and spiritual levels.

Faeries – Beings, in human form, who are connected to Mother Nature, depicted as clever and mischievous, containing magickal powers.

Frequency – Tones or sounds omitted from living and non-living sources, which may or may not be heard by the human ear.

Homeopathy – A healing practice that treats disease by administering minute doses of a remedy, which when administered to a healthy person would produce symptoms similar to the disease, thereby building up the body's natural defenses.

Manifestation – The ability to turn the energy of thought, whether from human or Divine, into a physical reality.

Masters – Enlightened beings, earthly or from the heavens, who teach and bring miracles to humanity.

Meridians – In Traditional Chinese Medicine, the body is divided into twelve energetic regions, each being associated with a different organ, identified by a specific colour and frequency or tone.

Naturopathy – A healing system which focuses on cleansing and strengthening the body through the use of fresh air, Sunlight, pure water, diet, massage, acupuncture, botanical medicines, rest, etc. all of which can help prevent disease.

Prism – A transparent object, often made of glass such as the pyramid Sir Isaac Newton passed light through to reveal the entire spectrum of the rainbow.

Quantum Physics – A type of physics which can measure what is unseen to the human eye, and has no limits.

Unconditional Love – The highest form of true love, a love which requires no conditions to be accepted.

Universal Light – The "all knowing" halo or light seen cast around the Hearts and crowns of Angels and Masters depicted in Medieval and Renaissance religious arts.

Bibliography

Ambika Wauters: Chakras And Their Archetypes: Uniting Energy Awareness and Spiritual Growth. The Crossing Press. USA 1997

Augustus Le Plongeon, M.D. (introductory preface by Manly P. Hall): The Origin of the Egyptians: Published by The Philosophical Research Society, Inc. USA 1983

Carolyn Myss: Anatomy of the Spirit: The Seven Stages of Power and Healing

Carolyn Myss: The Energetics of Healing. Published by Sounds True, Inc. USA 1993 (video).

Carolyn Myss: Sacred Contracts: Awakening Your Divine Potential. Published by Sounds True, Inc. USA 2001.

Carolyn Myss: Spiritual Madness: The Necessity of Meeting God In Darkness. Published by Sounds True, Inc. USA 1997

Carolyn Myss: Spiritual Power, Spiritual Practice: Energy Evaluation Meditations Morning and Evening. Published by Sounds True, Inc. USA 1998

Carolyn Myss: The Power of Choice: Intuiting Change in Your Life. Published by Sounds True, Inc. USA 2001

Carolyn Myss: Self-Esteem: Your Fundamental Power. Published by Sounds True, Inc. USA 2002

Carolyn Myss: Why People Don't Heal: Published by Sounds True, Inc. USA 1994.

Carolyn Myss and Norm Shealy, MD: The Science of Medical Intuition: Self-Diagnosis and Healing with Your Body's Energy Systems. Published by Sounds True, Inc. USA 2002

Dennis William Hauck: The Emerald Tablet: Alchemy For Personal Transformation. Published by Penguin Books LTD. England 1999

Garth Fowden: The Egyptian Hermes: A Historical Approach to The Late Pagan Mind. Originally Published by Cambridge University Press. USA 1986

Homer (translated by Robert Fitzgerald): The Odyssey: Originally Published by Harville Press. Great Britain 1961

Irene Dalichow and Mike Booth: Aura-Soma: Healing Through Color, Plant and Crystal Energy. Hay House. USA, 1996

Jacob Liberman: Light: Medicine of the Future. Bear & Co., Santa Fe 1993

John Anthony West: Serpent in the Sky: The High Wisdom of Ancient Egypt. Published by Theosophical Publishing House. USA 1993 (a previous edition was published by Harper & Row Publishers, Inc. USA 1979)

John Anthony West/ Chance Gardner: Magical Egypt (DVD): A Symbolist Tour – Volumes I-VIII

Louise Hay: You Can Heal Your Life. Hay House, Inc. USA 1982

Manly P. Hall: Freemasonry Of The Ancient Egyptians. Published by The Philosophical Society, Inc. USA 1937,1965

Manly P. Hall: Melchizedek and the Mystery of Fire. Published by The Philosophical Research Society, Inc. USA 1996

Manly P. Hall: The Adepts: Part One, The Initiates of Greece and Rome. Published by The Philosophical Society, Inc. USA 1981

Manly P. Hall: The Adepts: Part Two, Mystics and Mysteries of Alexandria. Published by The Philosophical Society, Inc. USA 1988

Manly P. Hall: The Secret Teachings Of All Ages. Published by The Philosophical Research Society, Inc. USA 1988

Paul Ferrini: Love Without Conditions: Reflections of the Christ Mind. Published by Heartways Press, USA 1994

Vicky Wall: The Miracle of Colour Healing: Aura-Soma Therapy as the Mirror of the Soul. HarperCollins Publishers. UK 1990

Recommended Reading List

Archangels and Ascended Masters *by Doreen Virtue*

Aura-Soma *by Irene Dalichow and Mike Booth*

Chakras And Their Archetypes *by Ambika Wauters*

Healing Through Colour *by Theo Gimbel*

Healing With Colour and Light *by Theo Gimbel*

Let There Be Light *by Dinshaw Ghadiali*

Light: Medicine Of The Future *by Jacob Liberman*

Return of Merlin *by Deepak Chopra*

Sacred Contracts *by Carolyne Myss*

Serpent in the Sky *by John Anthony West*

The Miracle of Colour Healing *by Vicky Wall*

The Principals of Light and Colour *by Edwin D. Babbitt*

Printed in the United States
by Baker & Taylor Publisher Services